The Extraordinary Landscape

To Michael

William Garnett

The Extraordinary Landscape

AERIAL PHOTOGRAPHS OF AMERICA

BY WILLIAM GARNETT

INTRODUCTION BY ANSEL ADAMS

A NEW YORK GRAPHIC SOCIETY BOOK

LITTLE, BROWN AND COMPANY · BOSTON

New York Graphic Society books are published by Little, Brown and Company. Published simultaneously in Canada by Little, Brown and Company (Canada) Limited.

Printed in the United States of America.

To my wife Eula
and our three sons—
Bill, Jay, and Don

Contents

Introduction

IT IS A PRIVILEGE to celebrate this achievement in art: the art of William Garnett, a man dedicated to excellence. In this superbly reproduced book he presents ample evidence of his powers of visualization and creation in a medium that is unique to our time—aerial photography.

The world from the air is, indeed, a new world, and visual/technical recordings of it, in black and white or in color, are breathtaking in their documentary efficiency. Many wondrous aerial photographs have been made: mountains, clouds, cities—a myriad of earth patterns— using infrared techniques, pseudo-color, and other electronic wizardry. All are interesting and excite the imagination; most are observations, accurate recordings of reality. We stand in awe of "the thing seen and photographed." Seldom do we witness "the thing seen, *felt,* and photographed"—interpreted in the added dimension of creative art.

Perhaps the first thought that enters the mind when observing Garnett's photographs relates to their abstract quality. I feel strongly, however, that his images are not abstract: the objective image of the lens is very real. He has in no way manipulated the basic images, but he has managed them extremely well at the intuitive levels. His control of his airplane, of the camera mechanisms, and of the subtleties of exposure is profound. I think of his photographs as "extracts"—imaginative, selective fragments of the amazing world unfolding beneath him. He writes of his colors being true to nature. Knowing of the limitations of color film, I would say that his colors are true to his *visualization* of his images if not to the objective reality of the subject itself. I am convinced that he intuitively selects, visualizes, and performs his creative works.

Garnett employs his highly selective eye in directing his camera—in a miraculous performance—to record what flows beneath him as shapes and patterns, values and colors. He pilots his own plane, thereby extending his image-control facility to an extraordinary degree. Truly, his camera has wings. He maneuvers his plane as he would adjust the position of his camera on solid ground, but with added physical freedom.

As a pilot, he can observe the development of his "decisive moment," that instant when the shapes of the world below join his perceptive eye in the formal expression of his art. His subtle visualizations demand this grasp of anticipation—the essential quality of perception that projects the world in split-second future time and space. This ability is shared by other great photographers, such as Henri Cartier-Bresson and W. Eugene Smith, who worked in intimate contact with humanity. There is no posing of an event in action, just as there is no stopping of an airplane in free flight.

Death Valley from thirty thousand feet is a vast and sobering sight: many thousands of square miles of arid mountains, deserts, and salt flats rolling to the shimmering horizon. Never, until the early decades of this century, could people have so completely scanned such a tremendous overlook of portions of this planet. Recently, we have been able to fly even higher—first to the borders of our atmosphere, then into outer space itself. Photography has returned miracles of observation to us and has broadened our concepts of the vast universe of which we are a part.

Garnett is fully aware of the glories of the world from the high skies, but he lowers his altitudes to gain a more intimate vision of the earth and its complex surface. He flies close to the dunes, to the farmlands, to the shores, deltas, streams, and the configurations of erosion. These are all recognizably three-dimensional, yet they are not the profiles of the world we are accustomed to seeing. It may be trite to think of his photographs as *revelations*, but that is exactly what they are.

We earthbound travelers are in direct contact with our planet's surface and are aware of its infinite configurations. Boundless beauty is perceived at close hand and from high mountain overlooks. The sublime as well as the evil works of society crowd upon us. We can smell the pollution of the air, we can taste the fouled waters—we can observe both the well-considered use and the spoliations people have imposed upon the earth. But we are restricted by our inability to encompass more than a small section of the environment at a time.

From the air our overview is greatly expanded; we can see the scars of the past and present on the face of the earth, the appropriate farms and orchards, the cities—well planned or not—and the untrammeled areas of beauty and wonder. The birds fly over the earth and waters, intimate with crags and forests, estuaries and the windy rookeries of shore cliffs. Garnett has photographed these and the land flowing beneath them.

From these images we will gain new realizations of the biosphere and its limitations. With very few exceptions, life is restricted to spaces within two miles above and below sea level—only one two-thousandth of the diameter of the globe! In this shallow vault lie both the miracles of life and the pollutions civilization has released—poisons that may seriously disrupt or entirely eliminate life, including ourselves. Smog is bad enough from ground view; from the air it is a desecrating veil. The clean fogs and clouds are part of the earth's reality; not so the coal smoke belching from proliferating stacks or the sinister emissions from millions of vehicles.

These could be controlled by man's ingenuity but are, unfortunately, encouraged by his greed.

We see areas of surpassing beauty that must be protected and preserved intact. Once they are destroyed they are gone forever. In a compassionate society, these areas belong to the world, not to the selfish few. Aerial photographs such as Garnett's show us, as no other medium can, the compelling obligation we have toward the future of the world we inhabit.

I am glad I have lived in a time of great artists and people who are concerned with the preservation of the world. I am certain that William Garnett is worthy of inclusion in both categories.

ANSEL ADAMS

Preface

THE PHOTOGRAPHS IN THIS BOOK are a sampling of the beautiful and unusual landscapes that abound in the United States. They show the changes in form and mood that characterize the various sections of rural America.

The primary subjects are the land and the natural forces that affect it—sun, storm, tides, erosion, even volcanic eruption and the heaving of the earth's crust into formations of awesome size and grandeur. To the extent that these photographs deal with places where man has left his mark, the mark is a gentle one, consisting mainly of the contouring of land for agriculture. My principal interest is in natural beauty—the spectacular vistas as well as the interesting combinations of color and line that can be found in all parts of the country but are sometimes only visible from an aerial vantage point.

To fly in a small plane and see the variety of beauty the U.S.A. has to offer is a thrilling experience. Indeed, with such splendor spread out before me, I often feel guilty that I am up there alone. No photograph can ever convey the total experience of peripheral as well as focused vision—the color harmony of sky and earth beyond the frame of the image, plus the textures of the fabric of the land, all set in motion by ever-changing relationships.

The opportunity to be totally surrounded by beauty is at once both inspiring and frustrating—frustrating because the shifting visual stimulations are constantly slipping away and because only a small window of that experience can be captured on film.

While some images may seem quiet and peaceful, recording them with a camera may involve extremely fast action. The moment when light, perspective, and design combine perfectly may only last for a second or two. It takes a small plane up to several minutes to circle and return to the same spot in the sky. By then, the shadow of a low sun may have raced more than fifty miles across the desert floor. Similarly, just as your shadow follows you when you walk, reflections seen from the air move over the earth's surface at the same speed as the airplane. The reflection of the sun or cloud that the aerial photographer wishes to incorporate into the design must be caught while the reflection streaks over the ground at a hundred miles per hour.

As in all good photography, lighting is the principal challenge and the key to the success of the photograph. Interesting subject matter becomes good design only when properly lighted and composed. It takes split-second timing in the air to arrive at a precise spot in the sky at a precise moment.

Achieving the desired result requires discipline and intense concentration. At the same time the aerial photographer is selecting the lens, taking the exposure reading, setting the shutter speed and f-stop, focusing, and taking the photograph, he must continue to search for other air traffic, reset the plane's power and trim, adjust altitude (to fill the frame for the selected lens), correct for drift, and check the best spot for a possible forced landing. Then, immediately after taking the photograph and another look at the sky for air traffic, he may have to look at the chart for exact location, write notes, reload the camera, check fuel reserves, check the radio frequency, and give a position report on his flight plan—all while flying the plane. All are skills you can master, with patience.

I acquired these skills separately—with instruction from fine teachers—then put them all together with constant practice and refinement. In the course of forty-seven years of photographing and thirty-six years of piloting, I have had a lot of practice: nearly a million air miles, close to seven thousand hours alone in the air as pilot and photographer.

Sometimes it is intensely hard work. In spite of this, there isn't a week when I don't yearn to fly for new photographs. It is still fun. There have been many flights during which I was ready but the elements were not. I photographed anyway and tried my best to make things work. Later I would study and learn from the failures. This practice has kept me in tune for that moment when preperception and proper mechanics must come together quickly.

Some of the colors, forms, and textures that appear on the following pages may seem extraordinary. If so, it is not the result of filters or photographic manipulation. The photographs are as true a representation as it is possible for me to achieve.

The images reflect only the peculiar combination of factors (location, angle of view, time of day, season, weather conditions, and atmosphere) that prevailed at a particular moment. These factors can sometimes produce results that appear unusual. For example, in a particular locale the sky might appear clear and dark blue, but the sun may be rising or setting, filtered through a thin cloud or dust that is a hundred miles away. This condition would probably result in golden or red light on sunlit landforms, while the sky above, in clear air, might fill the shadows with blue.

Water in a river or pond may be muddy brown, but by choosing a camera angle that reflects the blue sky, I can mix a color palette as surely as does a painter. A field of freshly plowed earth can be seen as brown (its "real" color) in direct sun, or it may take on a russet hue at sunrise or sunset. Facets of dirt clods can, from a certain angle, reflect the blue sky and become a soft purple. Spring grass may appear yellow-green with front lighting or blue-green with back lighting.

As you fly over the various sections of the United States, the changes in terrain are dramatic. Contrasts abound: Maine, with bright red vines on glacier-scarred rock; Florida's swamps; the "another-planet" look of the Dakota Badlands; the submerged sandbars of Cape Cod.

Farms are fascinating. Tractor patterns are endlessly varied and plowed fields have a beauty all their own. Rice fields filled with water make perfect subjects for reflections and color changes. I have roamed the sky many times to find a tractor at the right spot or a harvest at the right stage.

The Southwest is one of my favorite sections for dramatic aerials. The red rock formations, buttes, and mesas, combined with erosion cuts, become exciting in the light of sunset. Weather can create dramatic scenes, such as a windstorm blowing sand, or the rolling clouds over Navajo Mountain. In Indian legend this mountain is held to be the source of great thunder-storms—and I could believe this myself as I watched the clouds roll into upside-down skies and felt the fury of the wind as my plane rode out the shock waves. Small indeed is mere man in this country, where six New Englands could be placed with room to spare, and where within thirty minutes a small puff of cloud can transform itself into a spectacular sculpture with the volume of Lake Michigan.

When you look at these photographs of the great Southwest, imagine the level of the land before erosion. Think of the millions of earth-tons that have been moved ever toward the Gulf of California by such mighty rivers as the San Juan and the Colorado.

My hope is that you will be inspired by the beauty of our country and will preserve this beauty for yourselves and future generations to enjoy.

Acknowledgments

IT WAS Bernarr who took me, his kid brother, to the airport to watch the planes, and to the air races, where I marveled at the maneuverability of airplanes. He came up with hard-earned savings and shared the front cockpit with me on our first flight. The visual experience of that flight is indelible in my mind. I also give Bern full credit for my interest in photography. He let me use his glass-plate camera and built a darkroom for us to share. And he provided me with a summer job, which paid for my first real camera.

Earl Baird was a marvelous man and an inspiring teacher whose high-school photography courses taught me theory, craftsmanship, and artistic goals in fine balance. He loaned his personal cameras to me on weekends. We were close friends until his death.

I am of course indebted to the Art Center School of Los Angeles, where I learned so much about color and design.

I am also grateful to those who taught me to fly and to fellow pilots who passed on useful wisdom—especially Don Downie, who, as we reentered the commercial world after World War II, piloted me while I took pictures. He coached me with "stick time," revealing that piloting and photographing are feasible for the solo pilot.

The following people gave me recognition when photography—much less aerial photography—was not yet recognized as a serious art form. This gave me the added impetus, in the early days, to continue flying for many of the images that appear here. There was no market for them at that time.

Dorris and Fred Wright, dear friends since art-school days, provided me with a home away from home in New York. From them I learned much about color harmony. Their early enthusiasm for my aerial photographs spurred me on. They, together with Dick McGraw and Edward Weston, gave me courage to apply for my first Guggenheim Fellowship.

The John Simon Guggenheim Memorial Foundation gave me three generous fellowships to work in the air—in 1953, 1956, and 1975. The first two made important research possible (for pioneering low-light aerial photography in black and white with the slow color films of those years). All three grants provided funds that allowed me to continue my work in the field. Much of what I saw and photographed as a Guggenheim fellow cannot be duplicated because of subsequent changes in the landscape, and some of the resultant photographs are now historically important.

Beaumont Newhall, while curator of photography at George Eastman House, in 1955 gave me the first-ever one-man show of aerial photography as an art form.

Edward Steichen at the Museum of Modern Art in New York included my work in the "Family of Man" and "Diogenes IV" exhibits, then acquired twenty prints for the museum's permanent collection.

John Szarkowski, the present director of photography at the Museum of Modern Art, in 1963 provided my first art-museum showing of all-color aerials, in the form of projected images in the museum theater. (This two-man show included Roman Vishniac's color photomicrographs.)

Walker Evans designed the layout and wrote the prose for my first national magazine "portfolio," in *Fortune* (March 1954). This led to more than twenty years of *Fortune* assignments, crisscrossing the United States, Japan, and Australia for aerial photographs.

I am grateful to Time Incorporated, and to Hedley Donovan, then editor-in-chief, for his confidence in my aerial portrait of the United States, and for the *Life*-magazine contract that made possible many of the photographs in this book.

David and Sally McAlpin, James Mathias, Milton Halberstadt, Frances Johnson, Bob Byers, Jim Pipkin, Dick Stanton, Marge Bradley, Michael and Arlene Bernstein, and Jim Brodie helped by giving advice and encouragement through the uncertain early years of aerial illustration and during the preparation of this book.

Ansel and Virginia Adams have been so helpful. Ansel had the courage to recommend me for important assignments thirty years ago and now generously contributes the introduction to this book.

I thank Floyd Yearout, my editor; Michael Brandon, copyeditor; Nan Jernigan, production manager; and Amy de Rham. They have made the many details and decisions of book production as painless as possible for me. They have won their way into my heart with their concern for the execution of my desires in this book.

Mary Pettis was my able assistant through the first part of the book preparation. Rob Van Vuren helped with the final scramble in the darkroom. George Hildebrand, Geza Kadar, and Clayton Long labored to build the emergency tank that became necessary when we ran out of water for the lab while correcting reproduction transparencies for this book.

One man more than any other has kept me on track toward finishing this project. Lee Boltin has devoted a huge amount of time and energy to see my work in book form. But beyond his interest in the book, not a week goes by that he does not call long distance from New York or send a card from wherever he may be with concern for my well-being and for my photography. What a blessing it is to have friends and family who have faith in me!

I am grateful to people in research and production at the Eastman Kodak Company for the miracle of thousands of exposures on blemish-free Kodachrome film, and to the careful, brilliant people at Pentax for their innovations in camera and lens technology.

I appreciate the work of Stephen Harvard, who designed this book with great care for the design integrity of the images. Working with him was a pleasure.

I thank all my family for their assistance—in countless ways—in putting this book together, and for their appreciation of my efforts over the years. Prolonged field trips required patience from us all.

Deep appreciation goes to all those unknown people who carefully engineered my plane and its engine, meticulously crafted the parts, and to those whose care in its assembly gave my craft its rated strength and the integrity to serve me faithfully over rugged terrain, in temperatures from 20-below to 110-degree burning heat, through unrelenting, pounding turbulence, and yet to respond with delicate touch and ballerinalike movement in smooth air. Yes, to all you people at Cessna Aircraft, McCauley Propeller, and Continental Engine—I love you for your care. Thank you for three decades of safe, beautiful, privileged flight.

The Extraordinary Landscape

The photographer in his airplane

(*overleaf*) Blueberry bushes in Maine

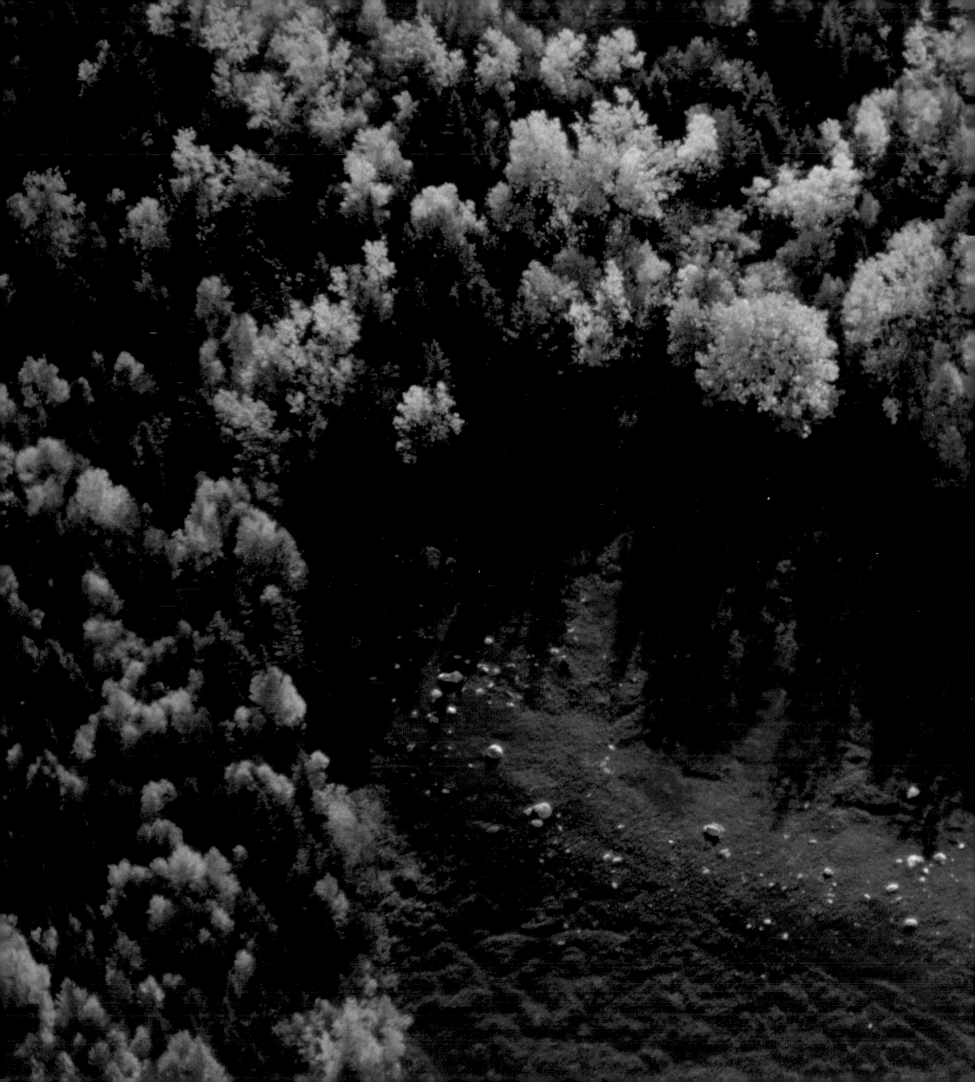

Near Gott Island, Maine

Rocks and vines, Maine >

West of Augusta, Maine

< Hatfield, Massachusetts

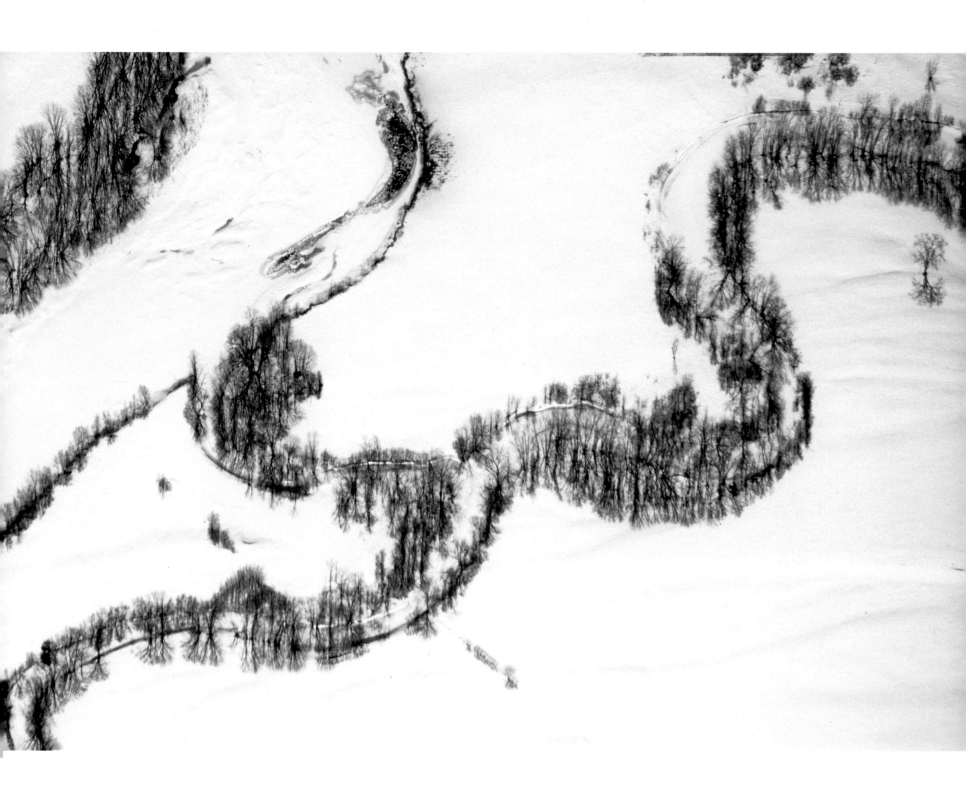

Near Bethel, Maine

Canoeists near Beverly, Massachusetts

Sunkhaze Heath, Maine

Sunkhaze Heath, Maine (summer)

14   Sunkhaze Heath, Maine (winter)

Sunkhaze Heath, Maine (fall)

Androscoggin River, Maine

Cobbosseecontee Lake, Maine >

(*overleaf*) Sandbars, Cape Cod, Massachusetts

Sandbar, Chatham, Massachusetts

Sandbars, Cape Cod, Massachusetts >

Sandbars, Cape Cod, Massachusetts

Low-tide patterns, Cape Cod, Massachusetts

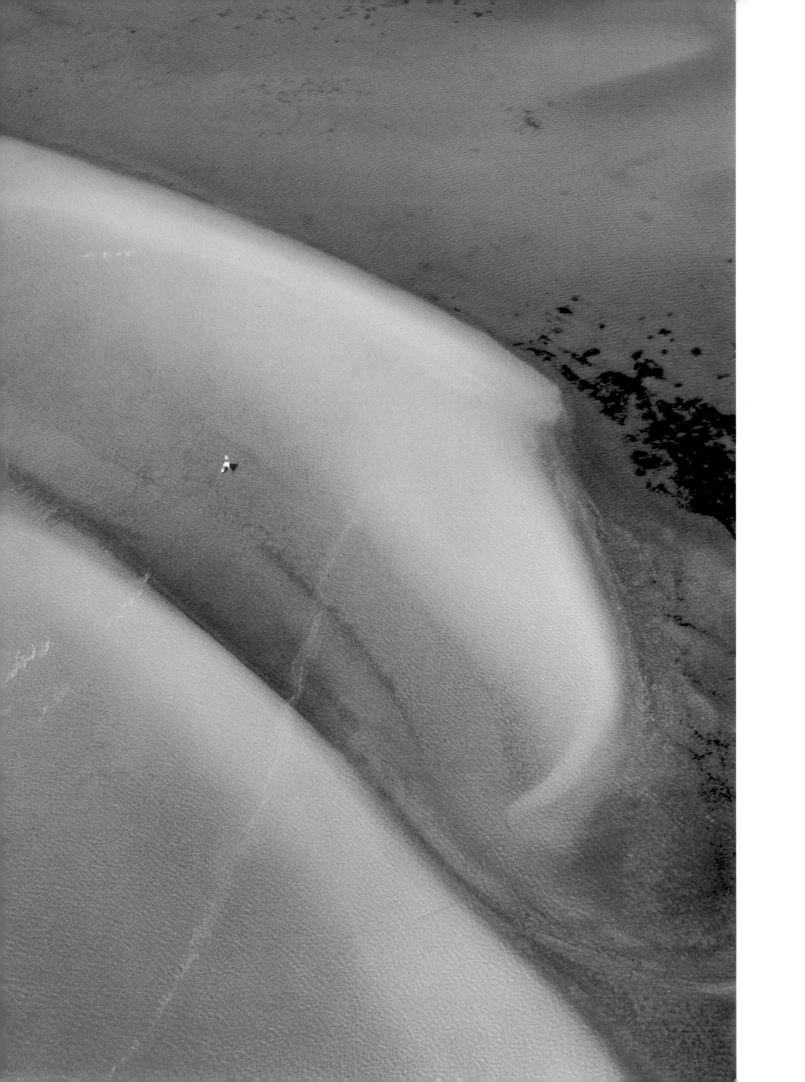

Boat and sandbar, Cape Cod, Massachusetts

< Sailboat, Cape Cod, Massachusetts

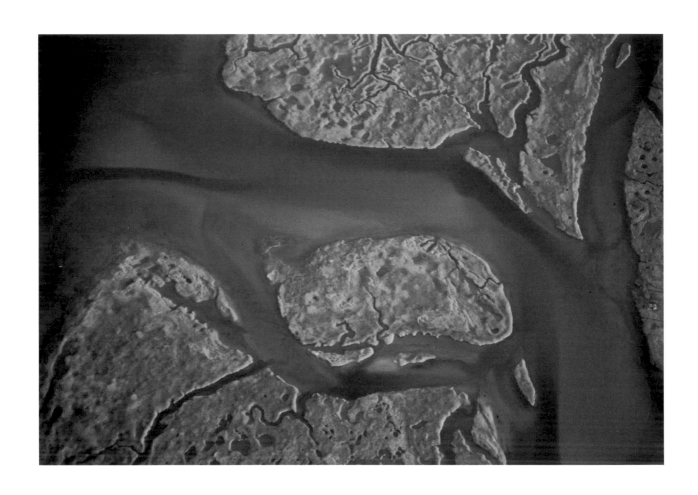

Tidal channels, Ipswich, Massachusetts

Sandbars, Crane's Beach, Massachusetts >

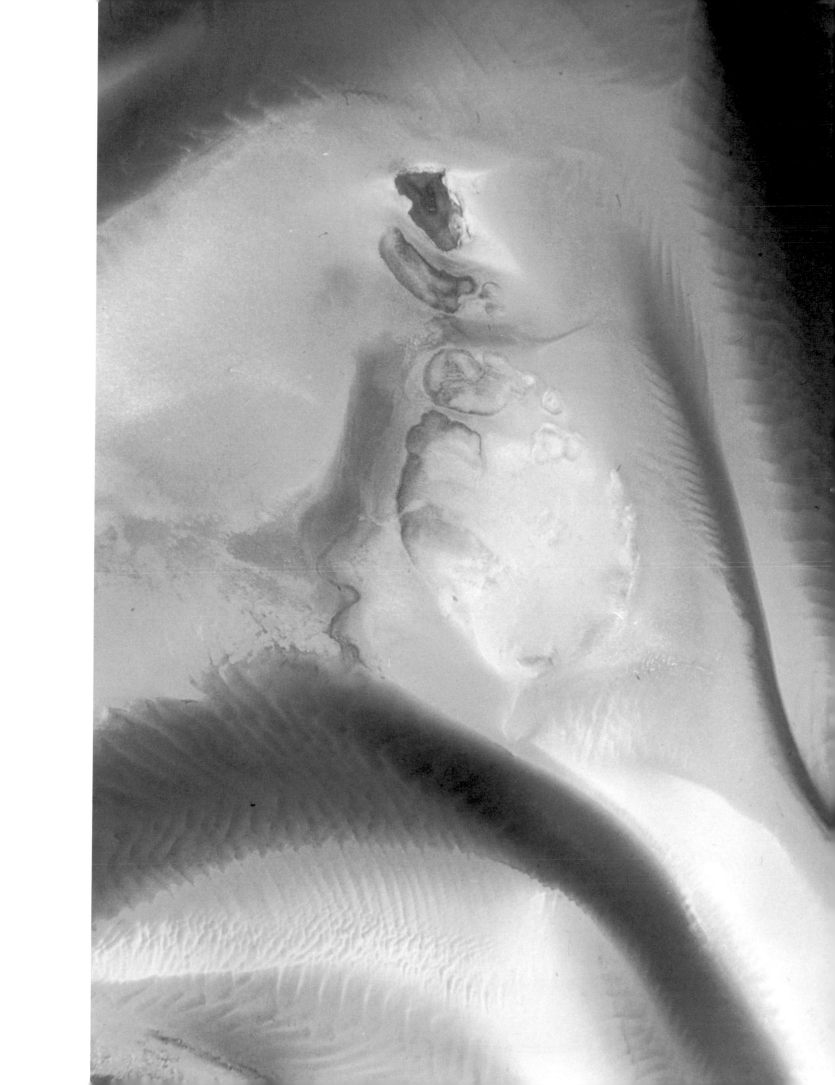

Canoes near Tupper Lake, New York

Virginia farm

Blue Ridge Mountains, Virginia

Strand near Savannah, Georgia

Cooper River, South Carolina

Florida everglades

Continental shelf off Florida

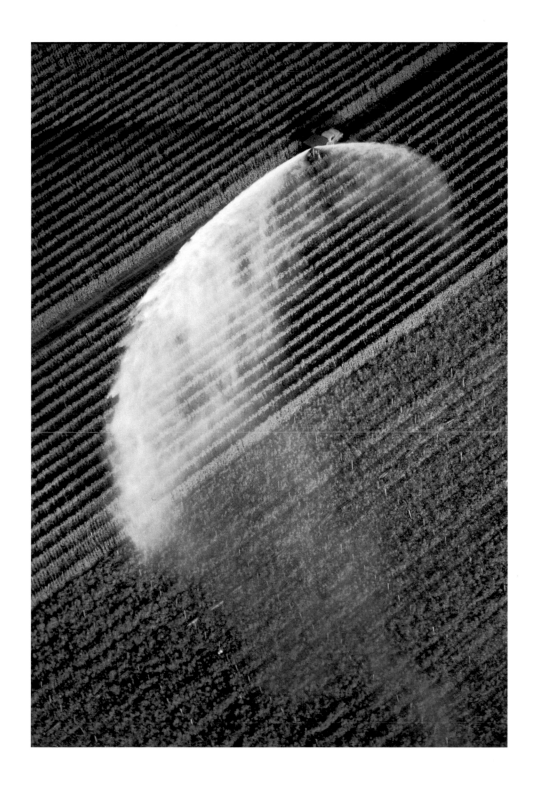

A sprinkler, Florida

Everglades near Orlando, Florida

Florida Keys >

Alligator pond, Florida Everglades

Florida Everglades

Pelicans near Naples, Florida

Big Cypress Swamp, Florida >

40

Everglades National Park, Florida

Ten Thousand Islands, Florida

(*overleaf*) Near Panacea, Florida

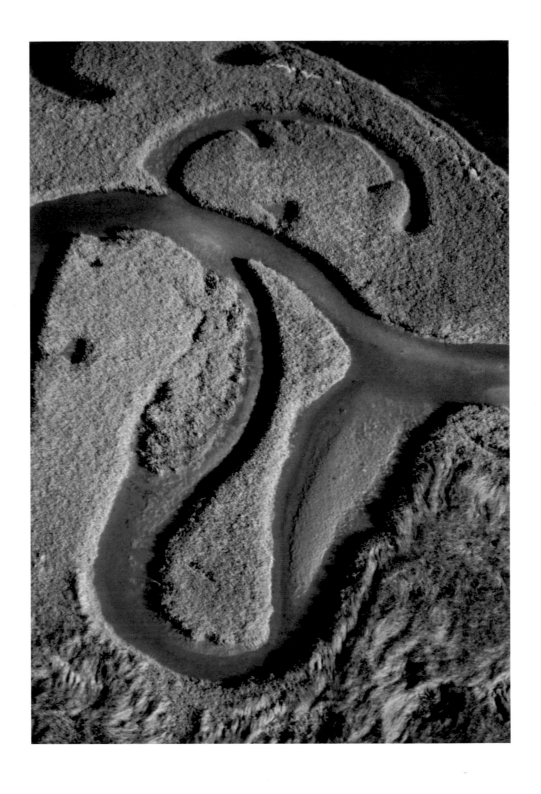

Tidal marsh, Florida

Mississippi River near Clarksdale, Mississippi

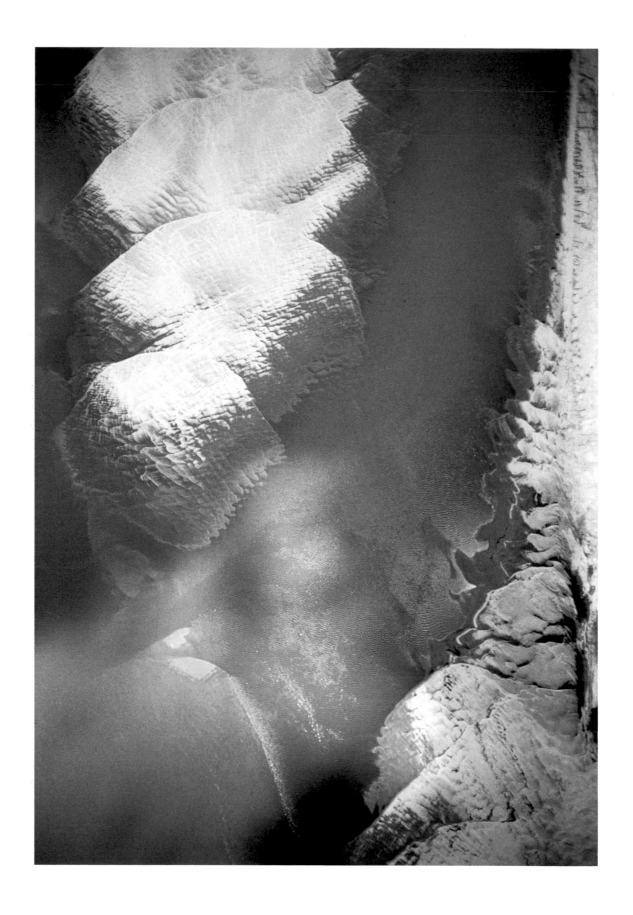

Mississippi River sandbars, Memphis, Tennessee

Mississippi River near Moline, Illinois

Shadows on a pond, Illinois

Near Prairie du Chien, Wisconsin

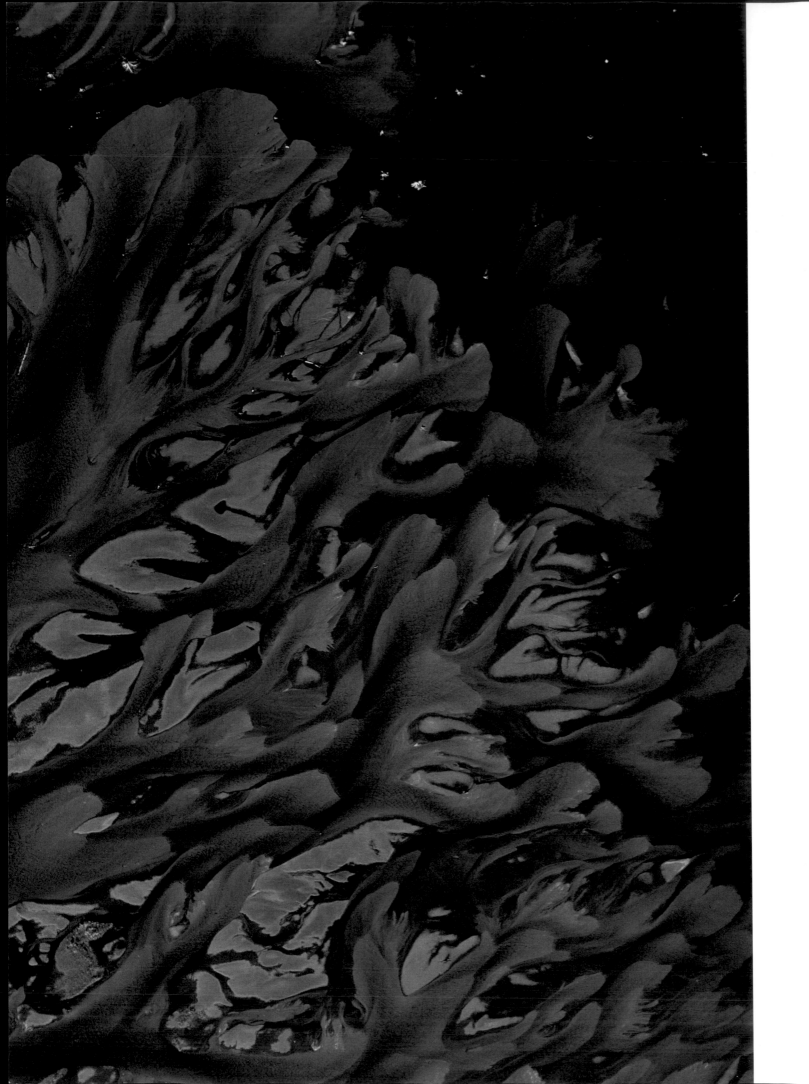

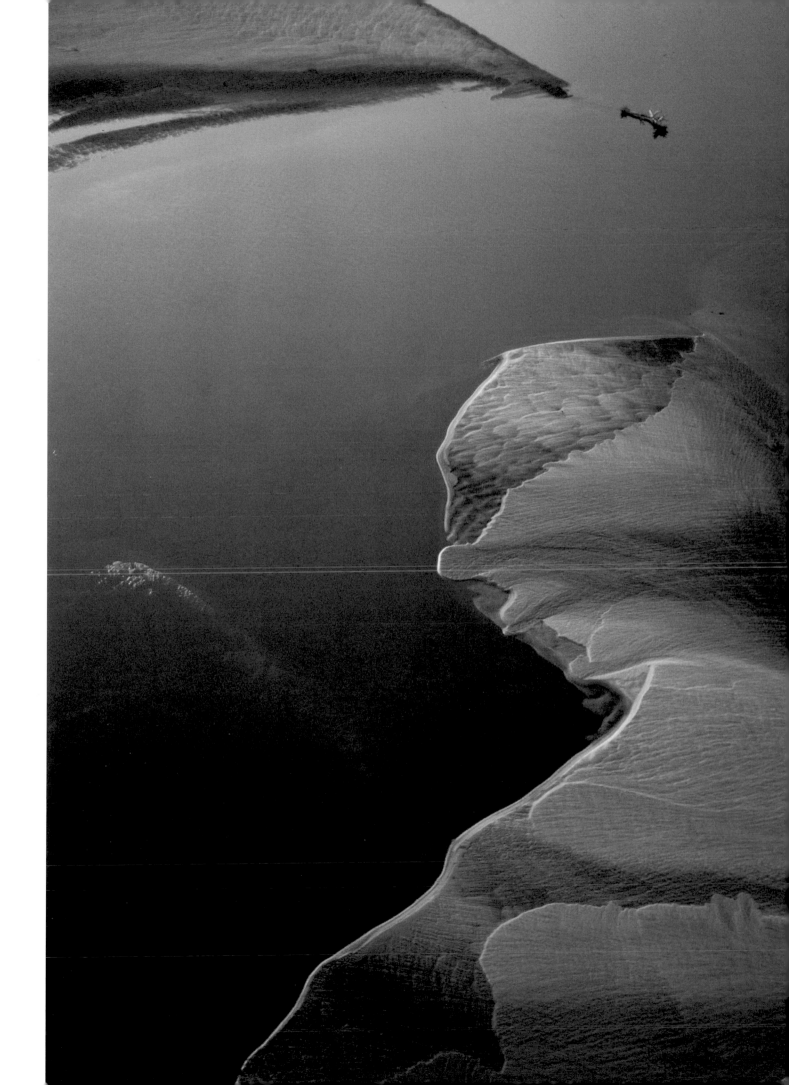

< > Sandbars,
Wisconsin River

Michigan farm

Lake in Michigan

Midwestern farms in the snow

< Wisconsin farm

58   Contour farming, Phillipsburg, Kansas

Tractor patterns, Goodland, Kansas

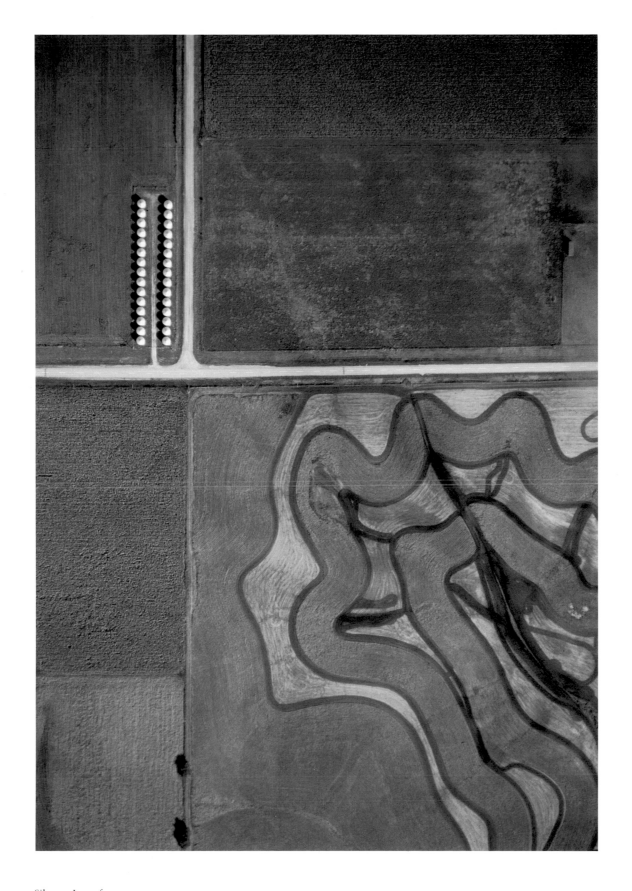

Silos on Iowa farm

< Iowa farmland

Strip farming, Iowa

Windmill west of Marfa, Texas

(*overleaf*) Sandhill cranes over Brazos River, Texas

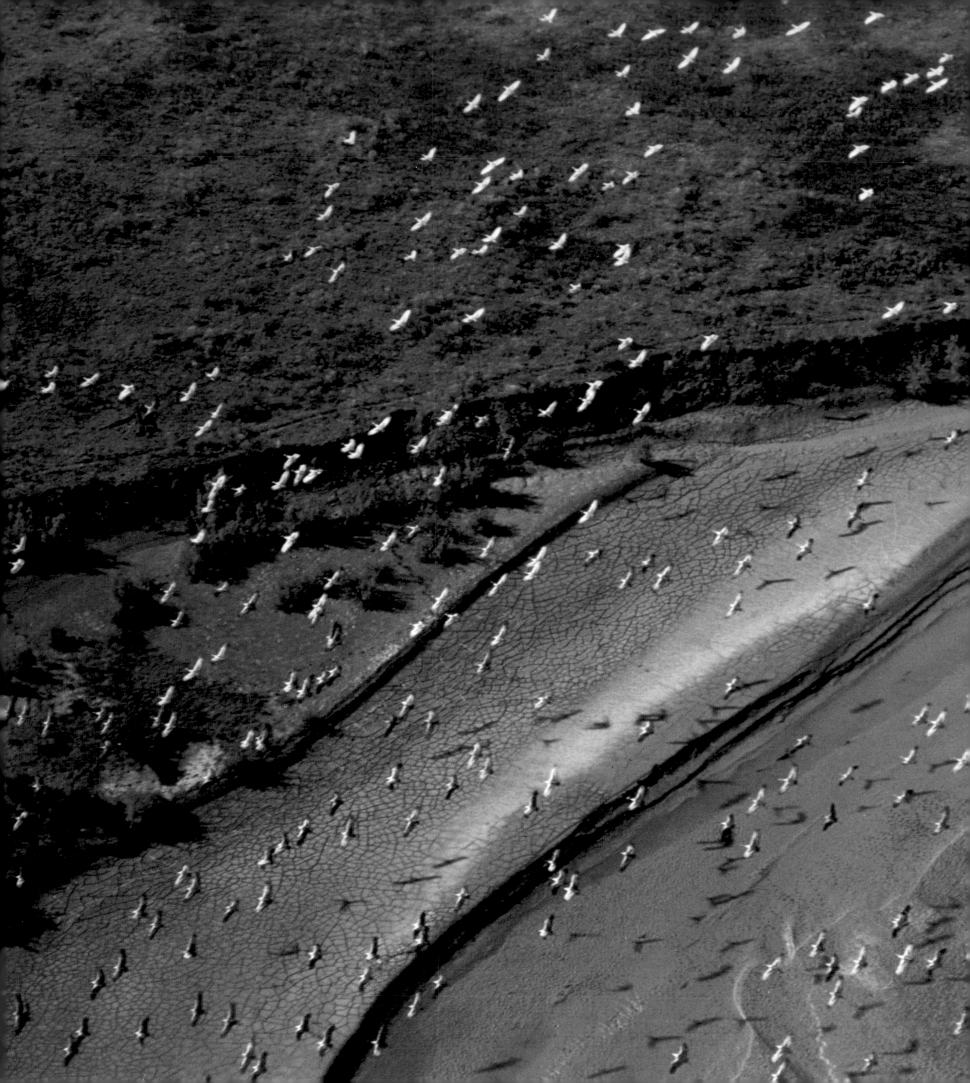

Detail of eroded butte

< Butte near Caineville, Utah

Eroded mesas near Gallup, New Mexico

Capitol Reef, Utah

Canyonlands National Park, Utah, in winter

Roan Cliffs, Utah

Arches National Park, Utah

Arches National Park, Utah

Delicate Arch, Utah

< (*overleaf*) Snow-covered cap rock, Arches National Park, Utah

76

Arches National Park, Utah

Arches National Park, Utah

Mexican Hat, Utah

Anticline at Mexican Hat, Utah

Comb Ridge, Utah

Painted Desert, Arizona

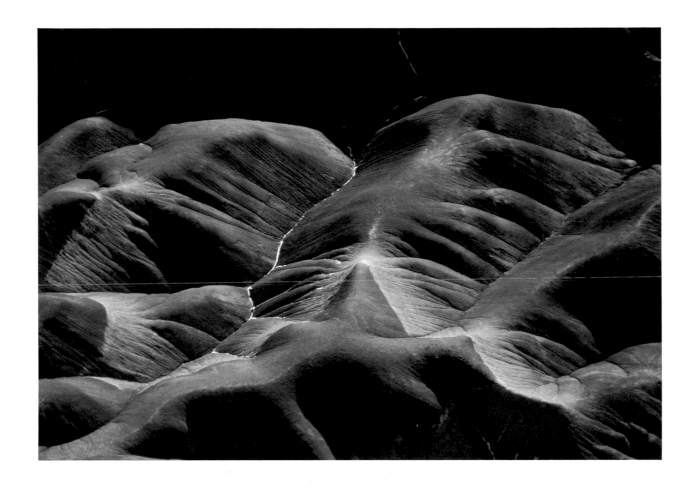

Painted Desert, Arizona

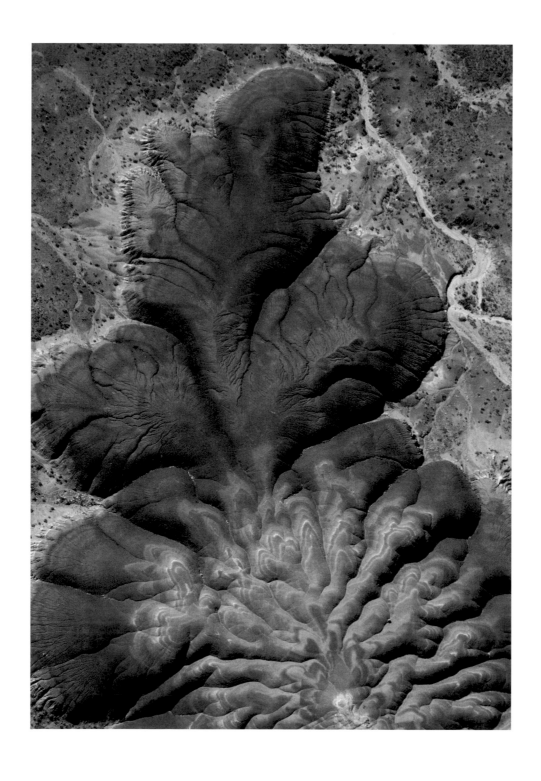

Painted Desert, Arizona

Sandstorm, Holbrook, Arizona

Monument Valley, Arizona

Monument Valley, Arizona

Monument Valley, Arizona

Marble Canyon, Arizona

Storm over Utah

West of Wahweap, Arizona

Lake Powell, Arizona and Utah
Bryce Canyon, Utah >
(*overleaf*) Earth, snow, and chaparral, Arizona

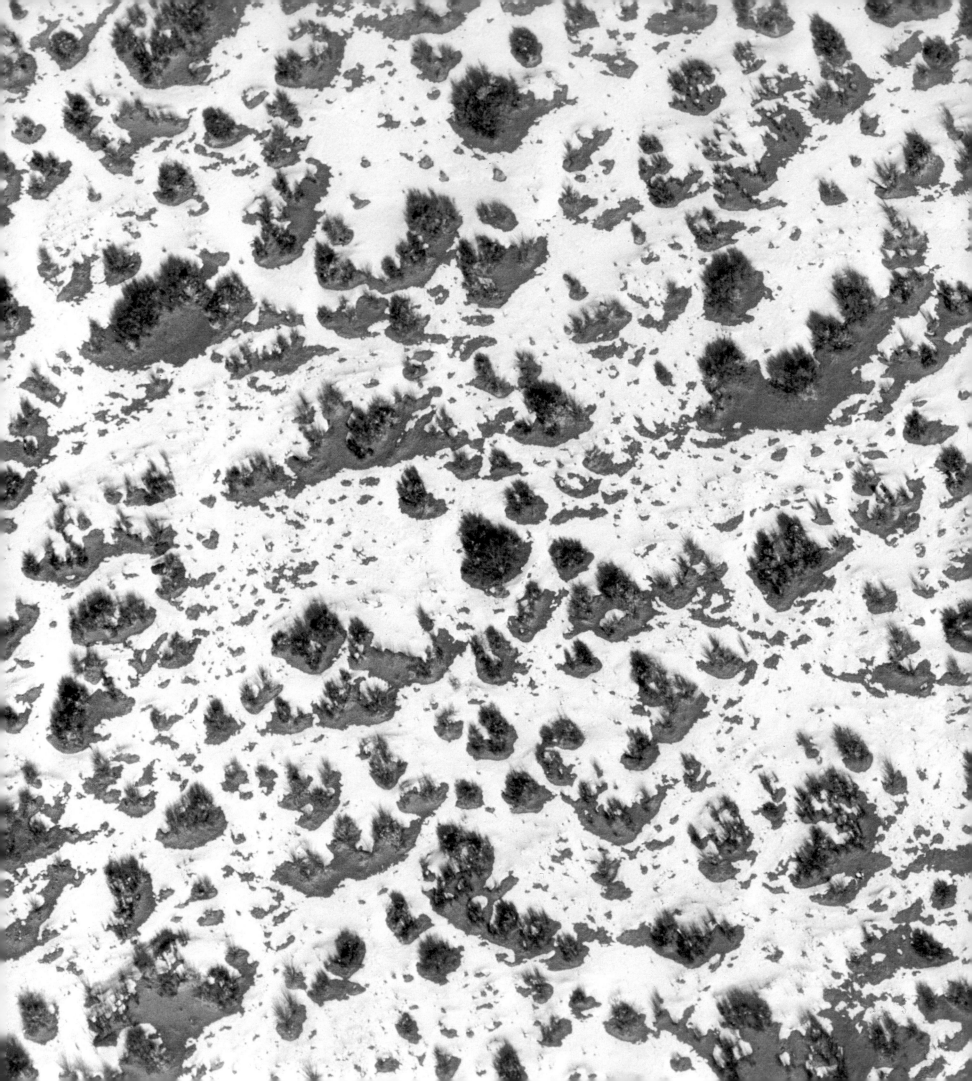

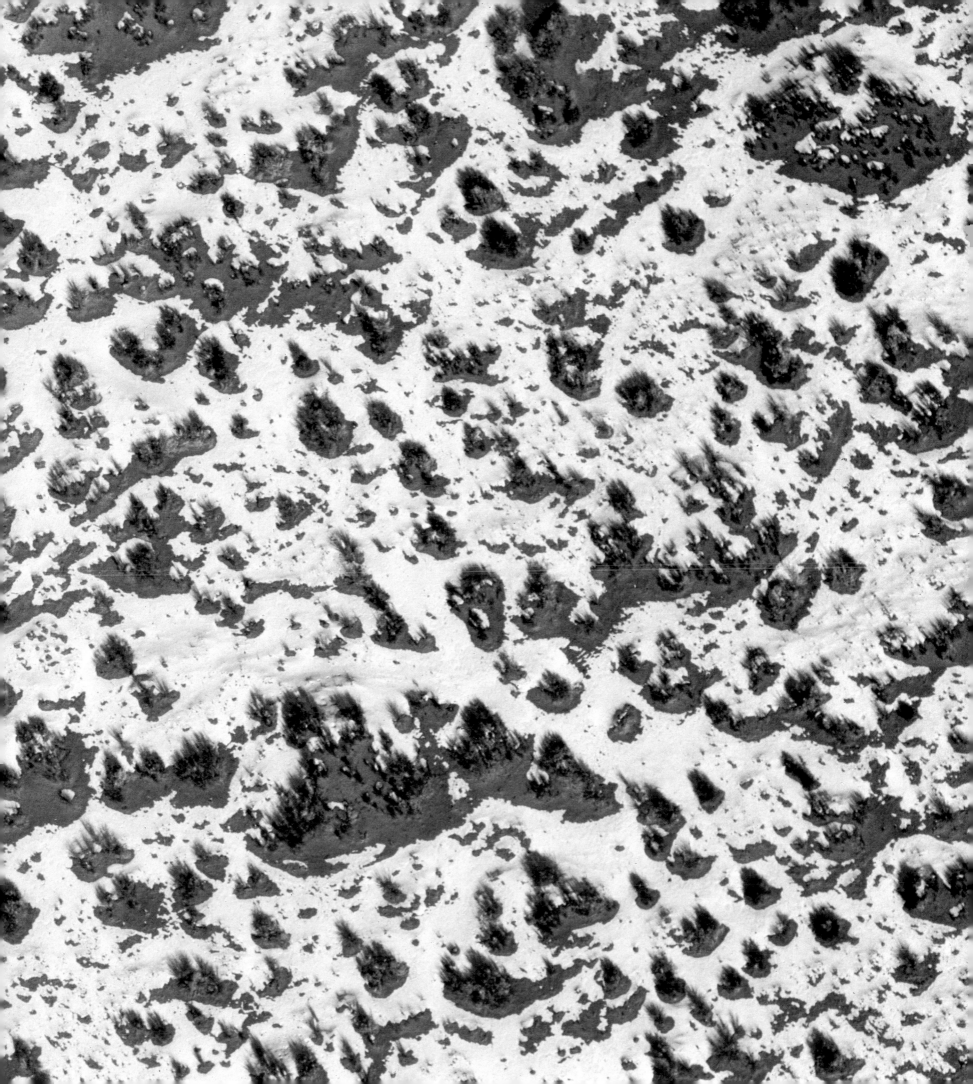

Hopi Mesa, Arizona

Eroded ridge, Hopi Mesa, Arizona

Cinder cone near Hopi Mesa,
in profile and from directly overhead

Detail of cinder-cone slope

Grand Canyon National Park, Arizona

Little Colorado River, Arizona >

Grand Teton National Park, Wyoming

< Exposed rock, Badlands, South Dakota

Jackson Lake, Wyoming

Snake River, Wyoming >

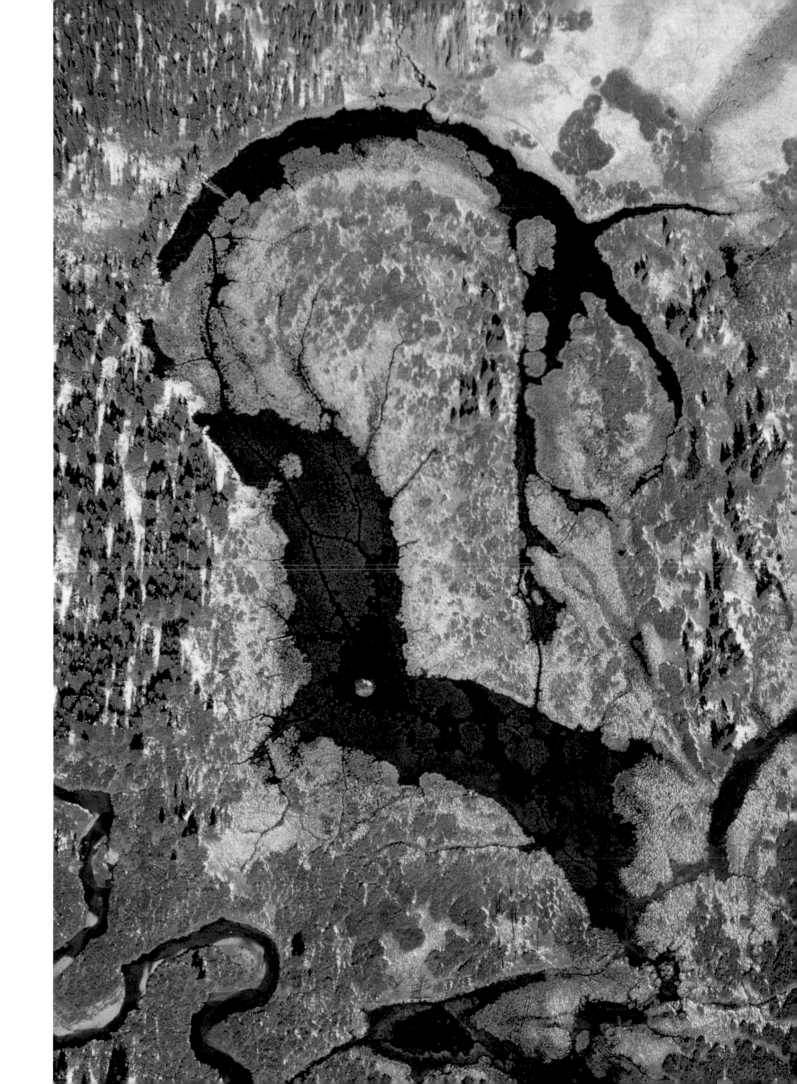

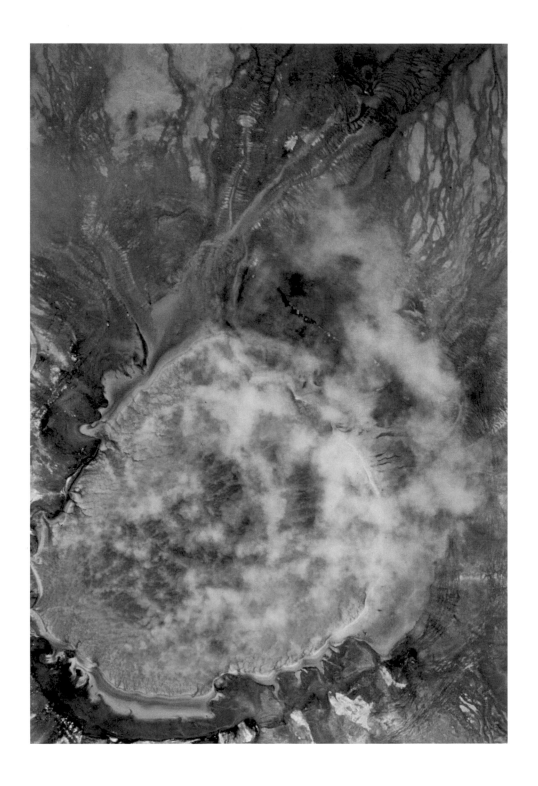

Geyser, Yellowstone National Park, Wyoming

Mount Katmai, Alaska

Mount McKinley, Alaska

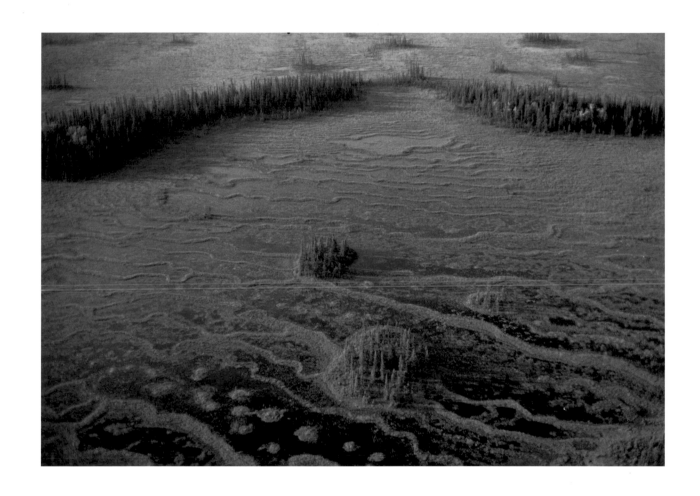

Muskeg near Talkeetna, Alaska

Mount Edgecumbe, Alaska (*top*), and Silver Bay, near Sitka

Slope of Mount Edgecumbe, Alaska >

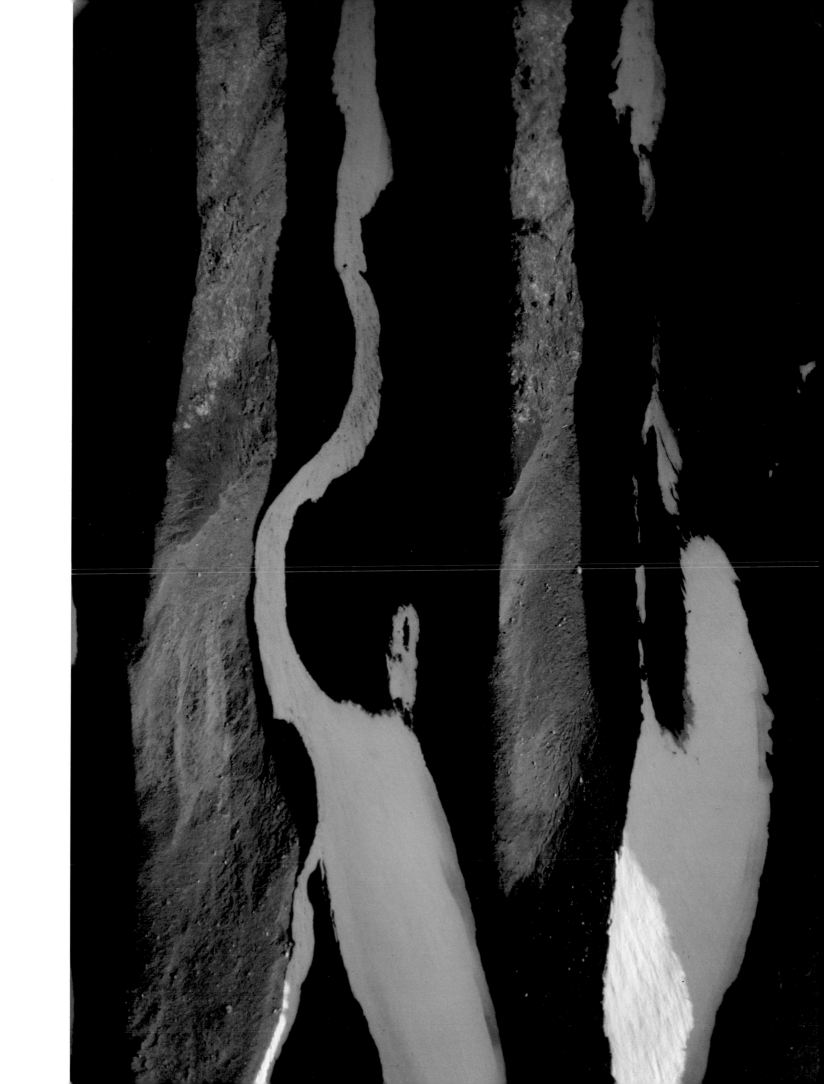

Northern Cascades, Washington

Mount Baker, Washington

Cascades, Washington

Mount Rainier, Washington

Mount Saint Helens, Washington (before eruptions)

Mount Adams, Washington

Wheat field near Pullman, Washington

Garfield, Washington

Near Pullman, Washington

Kootenai River, Idaho

Pend Oreille River, Idaho

Mount Hood, Oregon

Wheat farming, Tygh Valley, Oregon

Deschutes River, Oregon

Mount Thielsen, Oregon   127

Lava flow at Davis Lake, Oregon

Crater Lake, Oregon

Lava fields near Idaho Falls, Idaho

Upper Klamath Lake, Oregon

(*overleaf*) Mount Shasta, California (distant view)

131

Mount Shasta, California (near view)

Mount Shasta, California (detail)

Mount Shasta viewed from Tule Lake, California

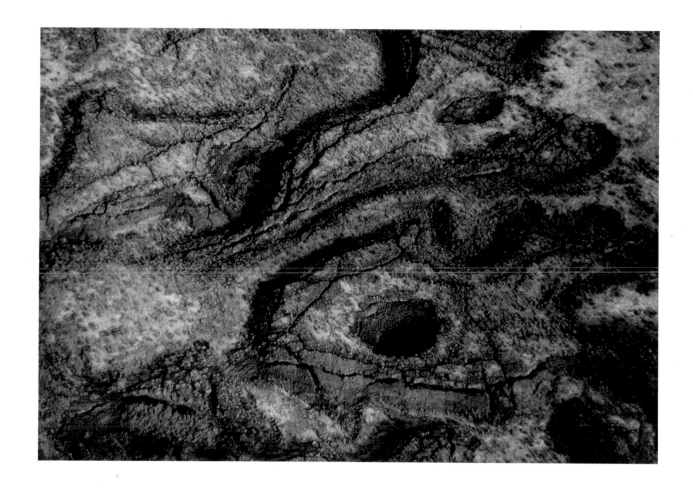

Lava flow, Tule Lake , California

The Sierra Nevada near Bishop, California

Ice on California's Crowley Lake

(*overleaf*) Timberline pattern, Yosemite National Park, California

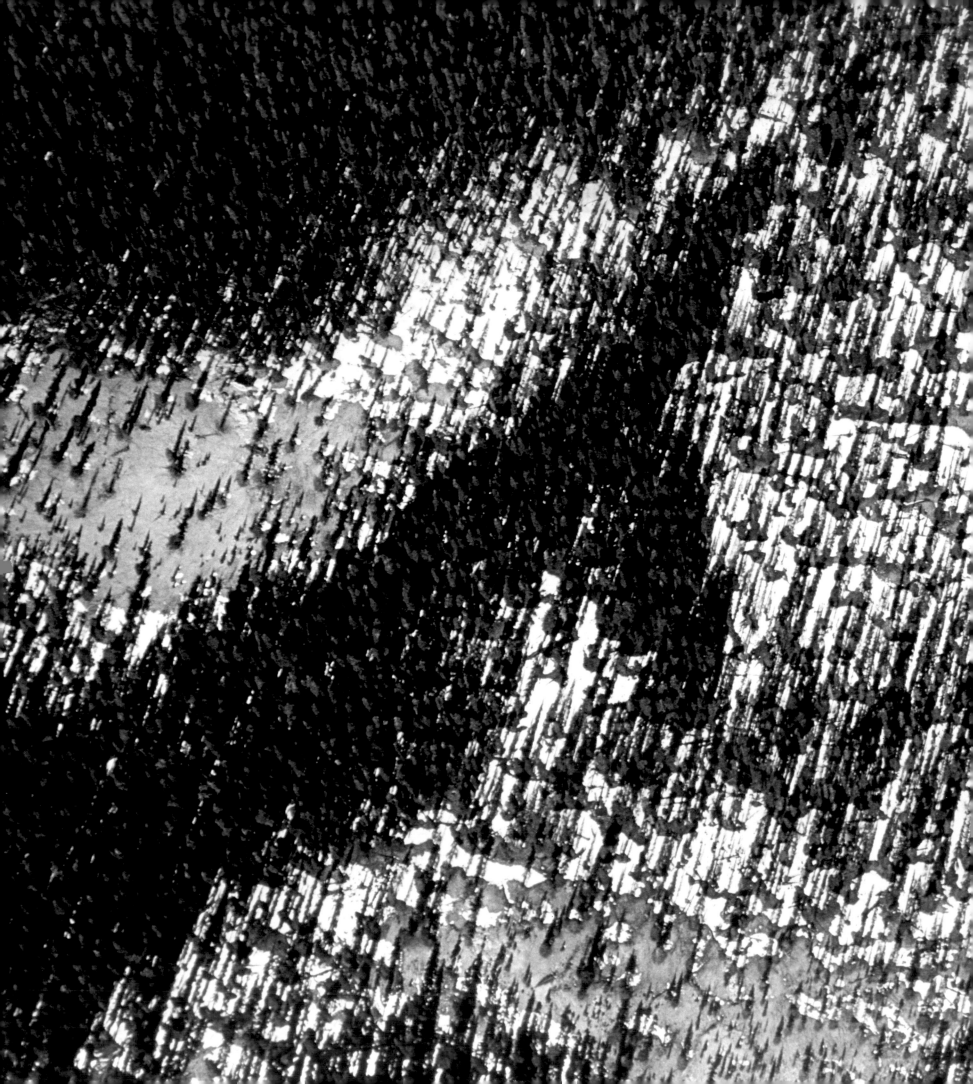

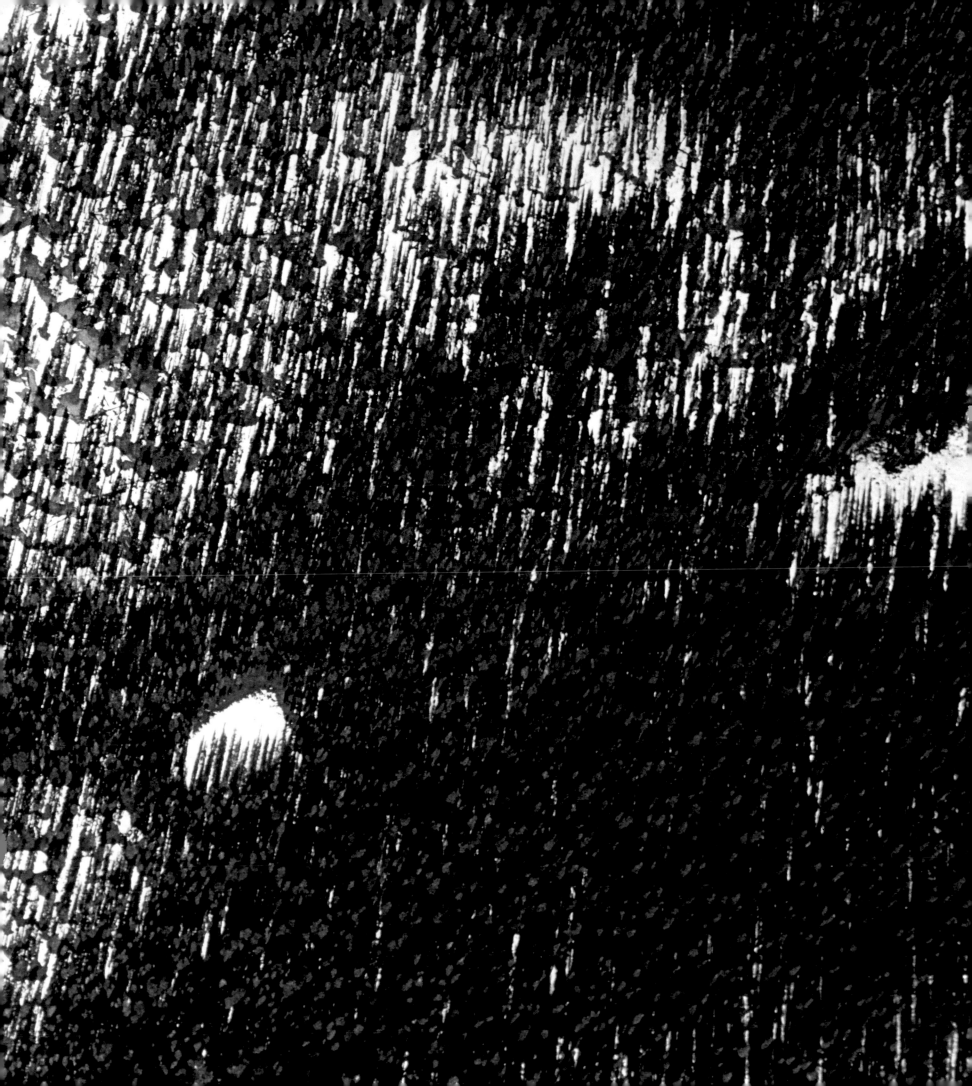

Mineral deposits, Owens Lake, California

< Owens Lake, California

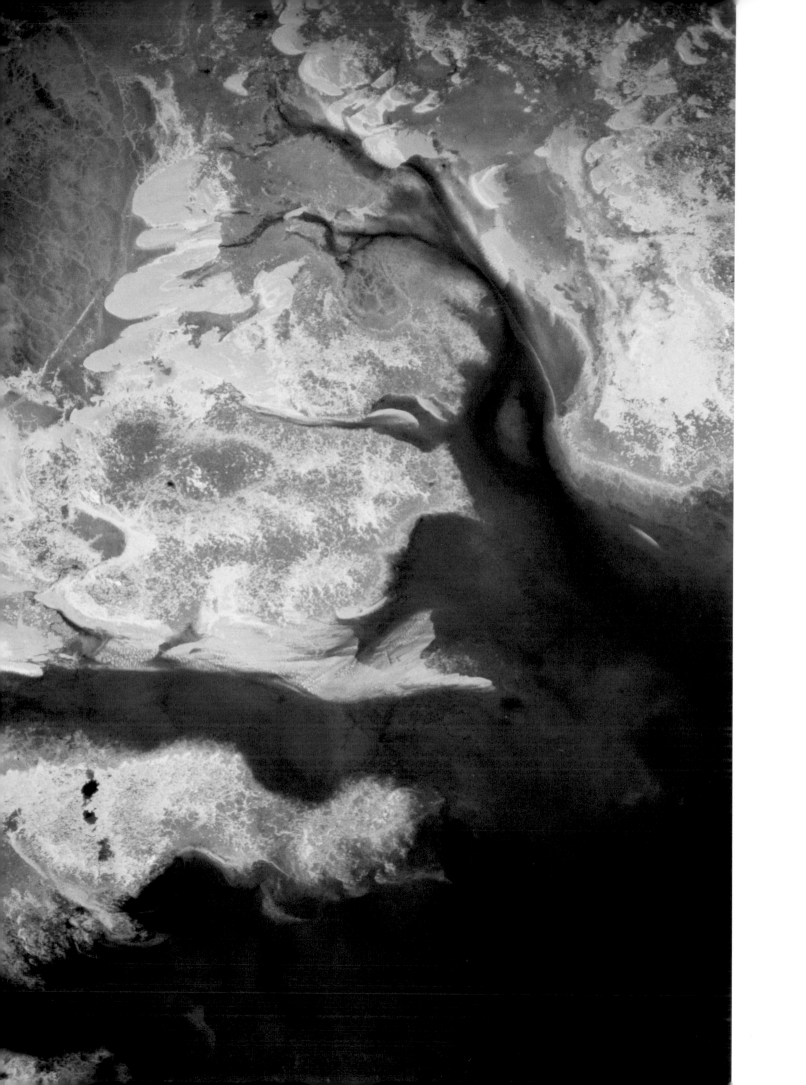

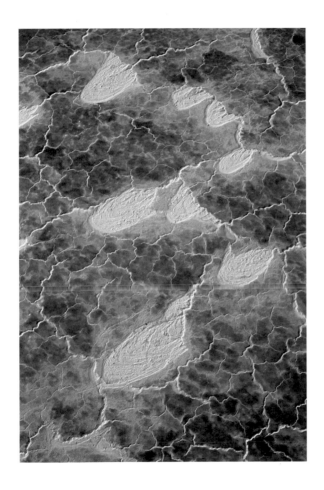 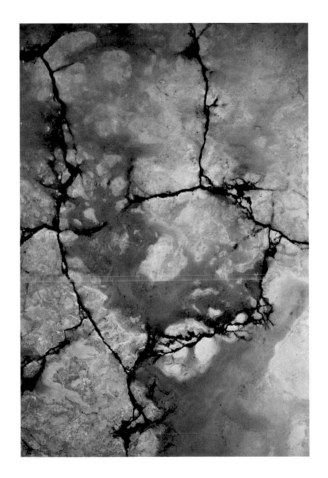

Three views of mineral deposits, Owens Lake, California

Inyo Mountains, California

Immigrant Pass, Death Valley, California

Death Valley, California

Sand dune, Death Valley, California

Death Valley, California

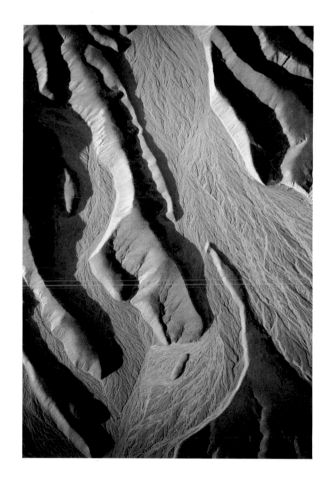

Death Valley, California

Tehachapi Mountains, California

Soda Lake, California

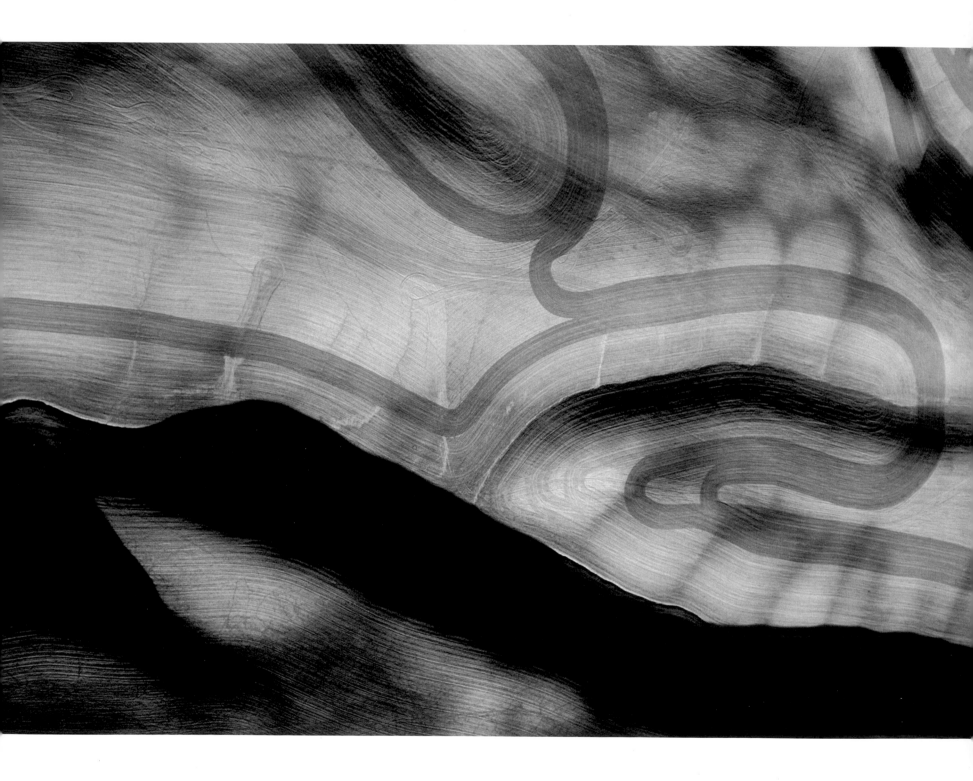

Plowed fields, Paso Robles, California

 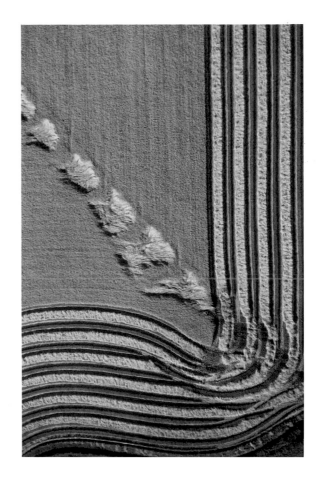

Paso Robles (*left*) and Sacramento Valley, California

155

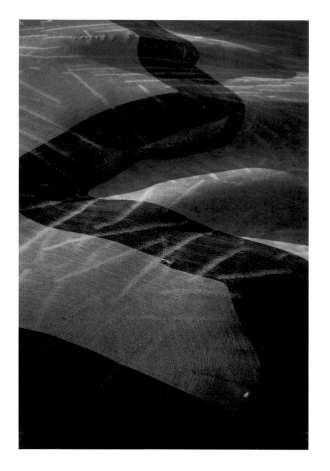

Montezuma Hills (*left*) and Hollister, California

Montezuma Hills, California

(*overleaf*) Geese at Colusa, California

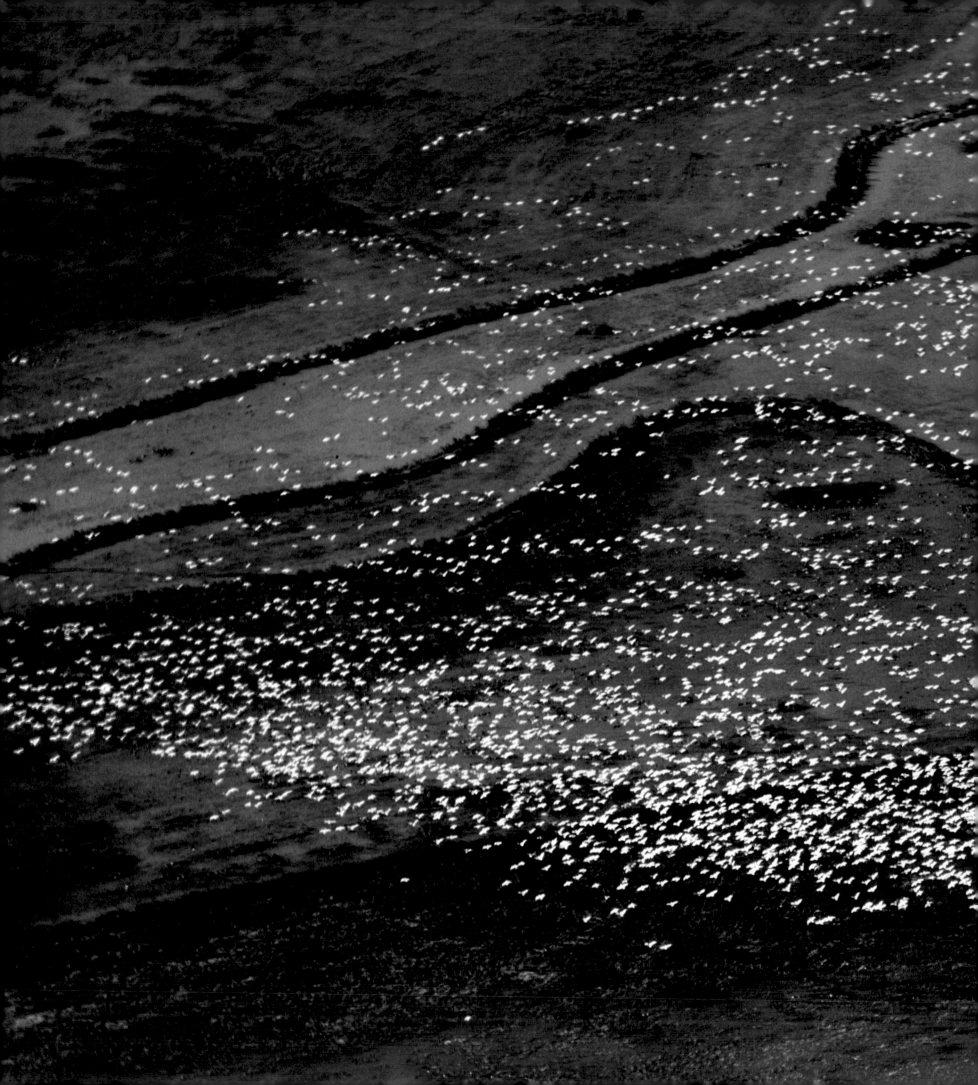

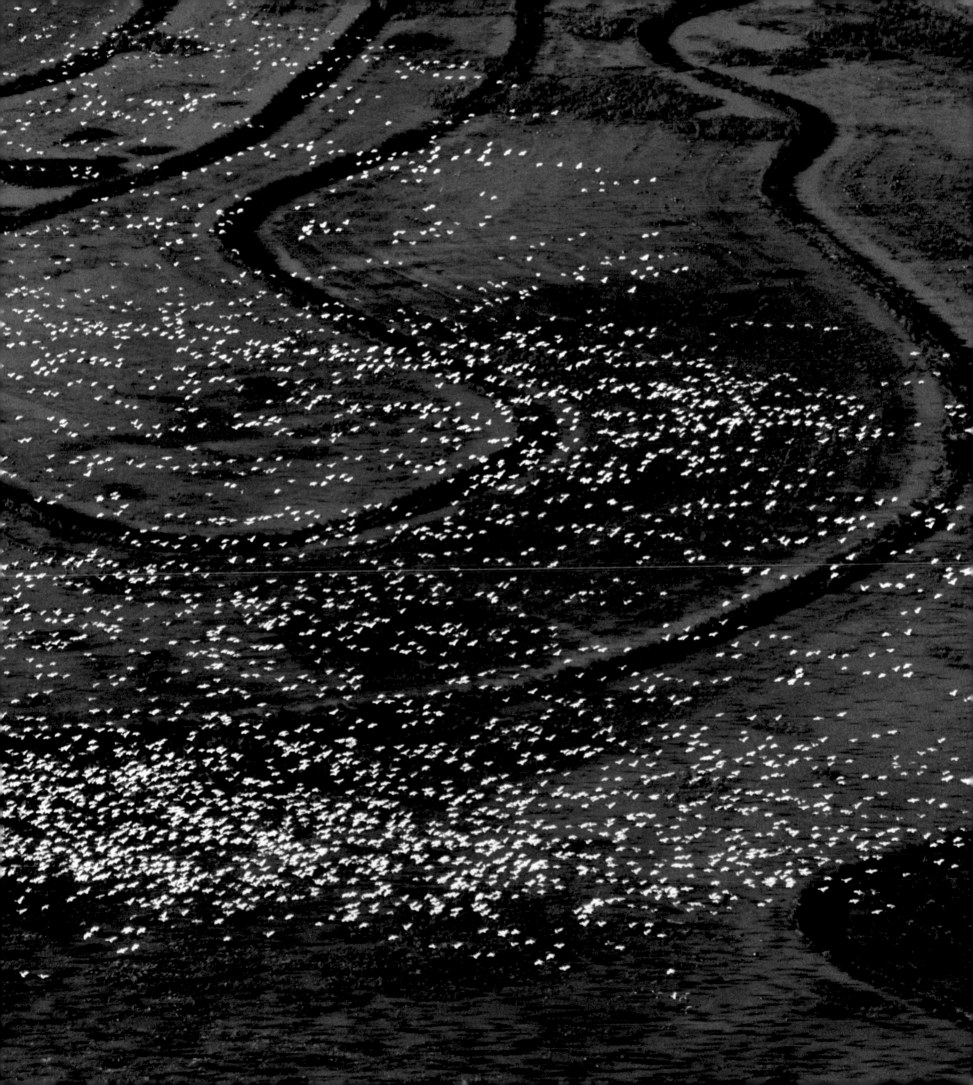

Rice fields (*top*) and windrowed hay, northern California

< Rice fields, northern California

Garapata Beach near Big Sur, California

Suisun Marsh, California

Morning fog, Napa, California

San Pablo Bay, California

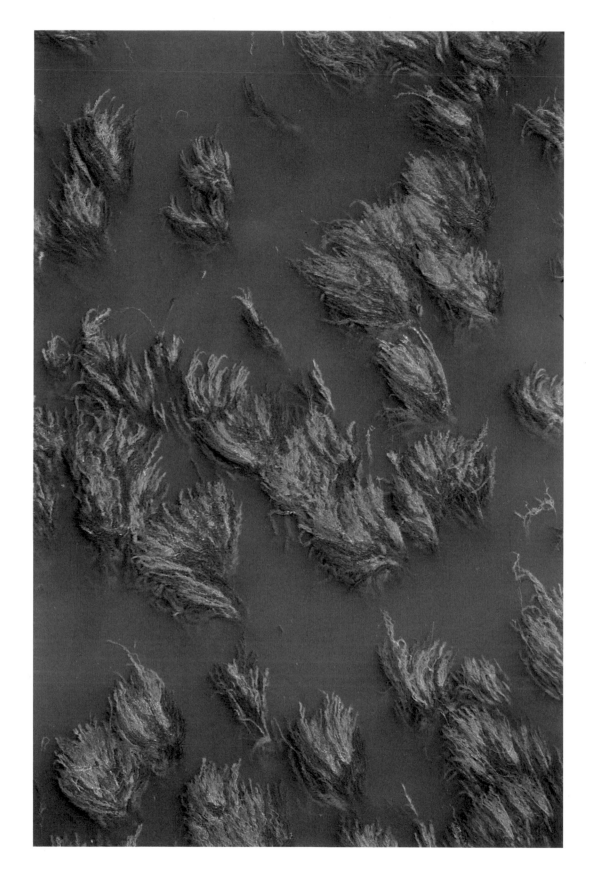

Kelp at Santa Barbara, California

Breaking surf, Molokai, Hawaii >

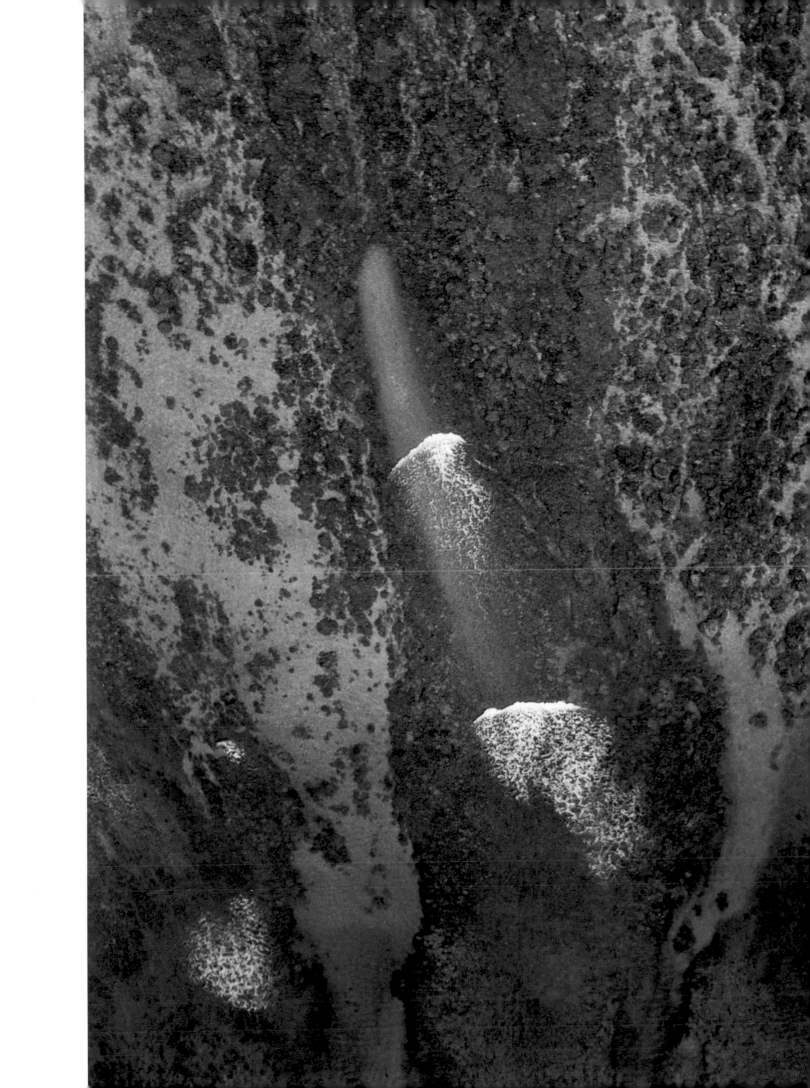

Hanauma Bay, Oahu, Hawaii

Coral reef, Molokai, Hawaii

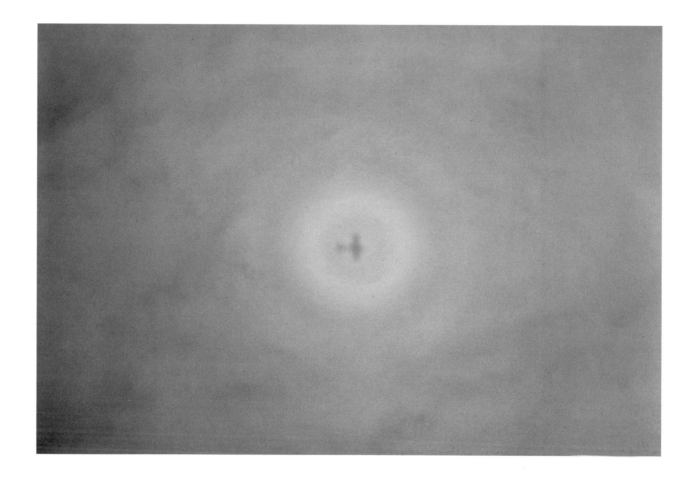

Airplane shadow and rainbow

Notes on the Photographs

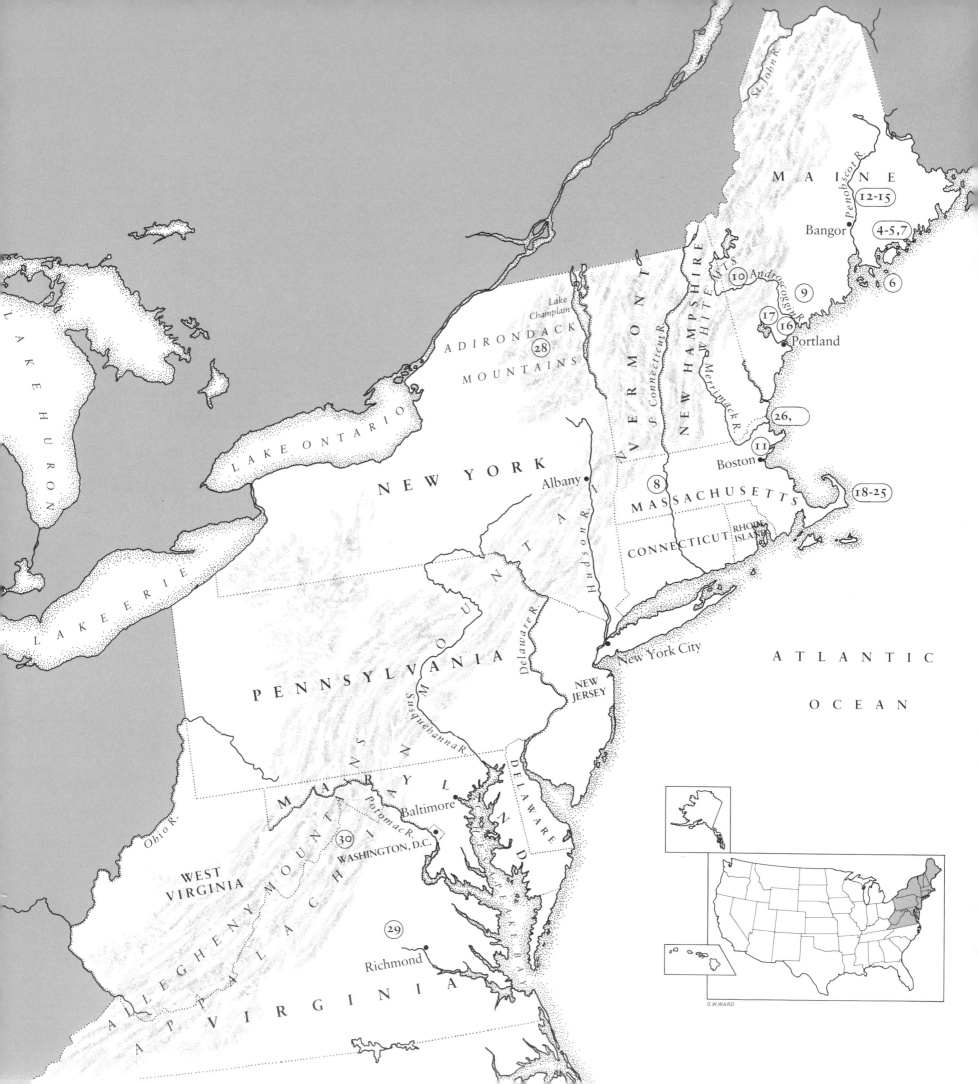

Maine to Virginia

Page 3 Flying my plane, a 1955 Cessna 170-B. Photograph by my son William Allan Garnett.

4–5 Open field of bright red blueberry bushes near Unionville, Maine. (October 1965)

6 The rocky coast of Maine in the summertime, near Gott Island. It seemed a miracle to fly over this rocky coast and see the lush woods apparently growing right out of salt water and rock. (1966)

7 Bright red vines with exposed glacier-gouged rocks, near Unionville, Maine. (October 1965)

8 Church amid the clouds, Hatfield, Massachusetts. As my alarm clock went off an hour before dawn, I looked out of the window and saw dense fog muting the motel lights. It was tempting to roll over and go back to sleep, but clouds and fog modulate light and mood and make fine photographs possible . . . so off to the airport I went. As luck would have it, the airport was on higher ground, clear of fog, and I was able to take off. It was discouraging to circle and circle, unable to see through the clouds. Then I noticed this church steeple, to me a symbol of New England. (July 1966)

9 West of Augusta, Maine. Circle and wait, circle and wait. As the cloud shadows drifted slowly by, I waited for the spotlight effect on the church and farmhouses in the distance. The reflection of the sky in the lake complements the beautiful fall color. (October 1965)

10 Near Bethel, Maine. Never before had I seen trees and their shadows so perfectly matched—like pencil strokes on a white page. This locked-in snow-and-ice landscape with trees outlining a frozen stream has remarkably subtle contours. The thin highlights along the edge of the stream are the reflection of the sun on the ice slopes of the stream banks. The temperature on this sunny day was close to zero. (March 1966)

11 People in three canoes enjoying the heavenly fall color near Beverly, Massachusetts. I hated to invade this peaceful scene with the noise of my aircraft engine, but I hoped the canoeists would forgive me for taking the opportunity to photograph this magnificent event. I couldn't help but wonder whether we might be jealous of each other. I had never been in a canoe in the midst of a beautiful autumn like this, and I wondered if they had ever been in the air to enjoy the splendor of this place from above. (October 1965)

12 Sunkhaze Heath, near Old Town, Maine. This pygmy forest, crisscrossed by what appear to be flow patterns of water, makes for a fascinating green-upon-green design. I wheeled above this comparatively small area like a gull hunting for food. With every turn there was a different texture, a marvelous reflection of color. I returned again, as you will see, to photograph seasonal changes. (July 1966)

13 A ribbon of the Sunkhaze Stream reflects the sky in this summer landscape. (July 1966)

14 The same site as on the previous page—locked in winter, frozen solid.

Trees are dormant, the stream is motionless, everything is quiet and traced in the most subtle colors. (March 1966)

15 The same hill and stream in fall trimmings. (October 1965)

16 Androscoggin River, Maine. Again the sky allows spotlighting effects on the beautiful fall color. (October 1965)

17 Cobbosseecontee Lake, Maine. A storm was gathering momentum, providing the dramatic sunset. Strong winds on the lake created these beautiful water patterns as downwind turbulence from the small islands reflected the exotic sky. This was the last picture of the day before I rushed for the airport and tied the plane down in a pounding rain. (October 1965)

18–19 On my first flight over Cape Cod, Massachusetts, the sandbars showing through the clear water off the cape came as a complete surprise. This photograph, made at a height of approximately 3,000 feet, reveals a sailboat in the upper right. The lighter parts of the sandbars seem to be above water but are not. I saw outboard motorboats and even sailboats travel right over them without leaving keel marks. On occasion, over some of the whiter areas, I saw people jump over the side and stand next to their boats. That was my only key as to how deep the water was. What appears to be sky in the upper portion of this picture is the deeper water channel within arc of the cape. (July 1966)

20 The surf of the Atlantic Ocean pounding against an exposed sandbar near Chatham, Massachusetts. (July 1966)

21 Submerged sandbars under shallow water, seen from about 3,000 feet above Cape Cod. (July 1966)

22 Another high view of Cape Cod. The large exposed sandbar at lower left affords a nice landing for a boat, which appears as a white speck from this altitude. (July 1966)

23 This photograph made from a height of about 600 feet reveals the low-tide patterns, water trapped in pools, and the sun shining on the muddy slopes of a Cape Cod tidal channel. (July 1966)

24 A small sailboat, seen from about 1,200 feet up with a telephoto lens, appears to be crossing an eerie landscape rather than floating off Cape Cod. (July 1966)

25 This small outboard motorboat was beached on an exposed sandbar in the Cape Cod National Seashore area. (July 1966)

26 Tidal channels and salt grass at Crane's Beach, Ipswich, Massachusetts. (October 1956)

27 Sandbars near the Crane's Beach inlet. The green shades of the channels vary according to the depth. (July 1966)

28 Two motorized canoes explore a wilderness waterway near Tupper Lake, New York. (July 1966)

29 Sunrise at a hillside farm in Virginia. Frost on the ground (in the shadow) reflects the blue sky. The sun on the brown plowed earth melts the rime instantly. (December 1960)

30 Detail of the Blue Ridge Mountains, near Woodstock, Virginia. (December 1965)

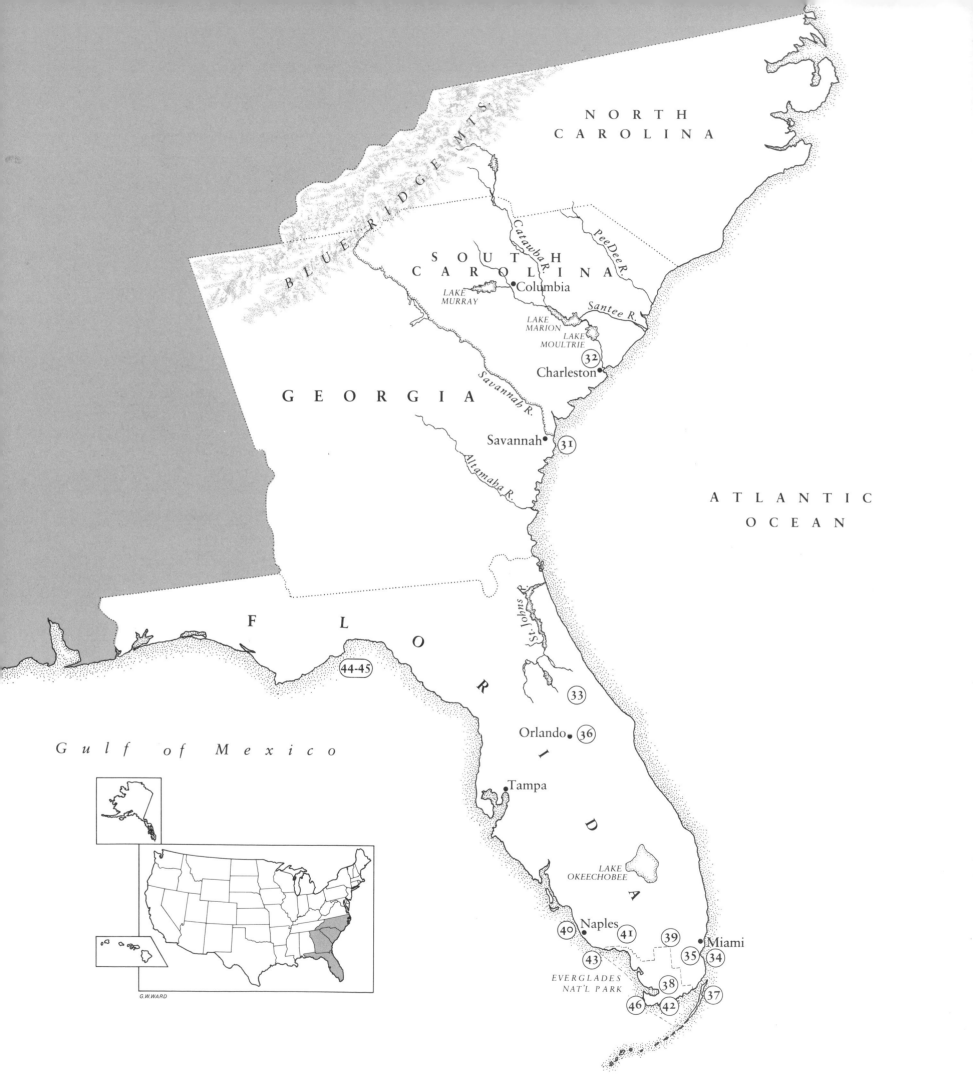

NORTH
CAROLINA

SOUTH
CAROLINA

BLUE RIDGE MTS.

Catawba R.

PeeDee R.

Lake
Murray

Columbia

Lake
Marion

Lake
Moultrie

Santee R.

(32)

Charleston

GEORGIA

Savannah R.

Savannah

(31)

Altamaha R.

ATLANTIC
OCEAN

FLORIDA

St. Johns

(44-45)

(33)

Orlando

(36)

Gulf of Mexico

Tampa

Lake
Okeechobee

(40) Naples

(41)

(39)

Miami

(35)

(34)

(43)

EVERGLADES
NAT'L PARK

(38)

(46)

(42)

(37)

G.W.WARD

South Carolina to Florida

Page 31 On the eastern coast near Savannah, Georgia, this amazing strand reflects the sun at low tide. (December 1965)

32 A lovely sunset is reflected on the Cooper River near Charleston, South Carolina. (December 1965)

33 A sunset over the seemingly endless Florida everglades. (December 1965)

34 This fine design was formed by the continental shelf off the Florida coast. My plane was 10,000 feet above the water. I saw boats that were quite large pass over the dark brown areas; the green areas are obviously deeper channels. From this height you see deep into the water. (December 1965)

35 The truck was pumping water out of an irrigation channel in Florida and spraying it with a large rotating sprinkler. It was great sport trying to synchronize my circling around this beautiful sight in order to catch the spectrum in the spray. Since I was circling at eighty to a hundred miles per hour and the sprinkler was rotating all the while, the angle of reflection was constantly changing. The rainbow occurred only twice as I flew a complete circle and each time was visible for only a fraction of a second. (April 1966)

36 The designs are endless in the everglades of Florida. I photographed this scene near Orlando. The ponds partly reflect blue sky, partly clouds. (December 1965)

37 This long view of the Florida Keys was made from 10,000 feet above the water. The clouds were at 8,000 feet, giving a lovely sense of scale and the third dimension as I moved slowly over the islands. (December 1965)

38 Flying in close at about 500 to 600 feet above the swamps, I caught the rich vegetation and undergrowth in this typical alligator pond twenty miles northeast of Flamingo, Florida, in the Everglades National Park. (December 1965)

39 The Everglades, thirty-five miles west of Miami. (December 1965)

40 This nice formation of white pelicans paid no attention to me as I flew at a height of about 400 feet over the shallow waters on the west coast of Florida near Naples. (April 1966)

41 Big Cypress Swamp, north of Ochopee, Florida. Made from an altitude of about 1,500 feet, this photograph captures the sweep and intricate designs of the cypress forest. (December 1965)

42 Cloud reflections in the Everglades National Park near Flamingo. The shallow water was very calm and mirrored the type of day. A gentle puff of wind made the strange pattern on the surface. (April 1966)

43 Ten Thousand Islands area, off the west coast of Florida, near Naples. (December 1965)

44–45 Near Panacea, Florida. The lighter sandbars were above water. (May 1966)

46 This detail made from about 300 feet in the air shows the grasses of a tidal marsh in Florida and the typical oxbow of a meandering stream. The stream is but a few feet wide. (May 1966)

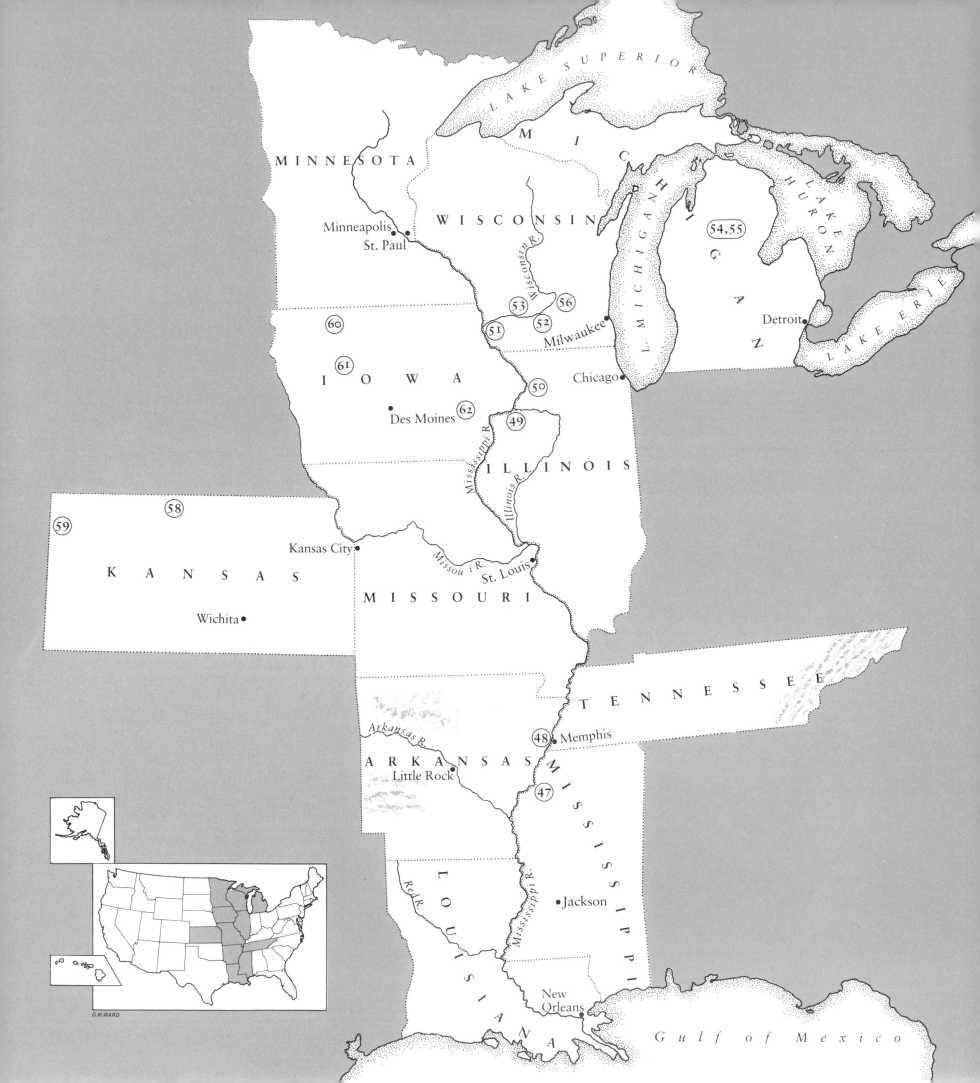

LAKE SUPERIOR

MINNESOTA

WISCONSIN

MICHIGAN

LAKE HURON

LAKE ERIE

Minneapolis

St. Paul

Wisconsin R.

54,55

53

56

51

52

Milwaukee

L. MICHIGAN

60

Detroit

IOWA

61

50

Chicago

Des Moines

62

49

Mississippi R.

ILLINOIS

Illinois R.

58

59

Kansas City

Missouri R.

St. Louis

KANSAS

MISSOURI

Wichita

TENNESSEE

Arkansas R.

48

Memphis

ARKANSAS

Little Rock

47

MISSISSIPPI

Red R.

LOUISIANA

Jackson

Mississippi R.

New
Orleans

Gulf of Mexico

G.W.WARD

Mississippi to Michigan

Page 47 The view from 17,000 feet above Clarksdale, Mississippi. I could see over a hundred miles of oxbows along the great Mississippi River. Note the similarity of the design to the Florida detail on the facing page. (January 1964)

48 Farther north up the Mississippi River, I found these sandbars right at the city limits of Memphis, Tennessee. A mottled cloudy sky allowed a little spot of sun to filter through and reveal the "true" color of the muddy Mississippi. The surface reflection of a hole in the clouds turned that same water blue in part of this photograph. The shading variations on the sandbars were caused by gradations in water depth. The lightest parts were above water, and the color darkened as the depth increased. (1957)

49 A big jump up the Mississippi, to the west of Moline, Illinois. (August 1968)

50 A backwater pond along the Mississippi, south of Savanna, Illinois. The camera was pointed steeply down, aimed at tree shadows, algae, and pollen in the water. (August 1968)

51 Islands on the Mississippi close to its confluence with the Wisconsin River near Prairie du Chien, Wisconsin. The coloring and type of sky are reflected in the water. (August 1968)

52, 53 Sandbars in the Wisconsin River. (Both August 1968)

54 A single yellow tree amid the green of Michigan's Lower Peninsula. (October 1967)

55 An early morning fisherman returning to port in Michigan. (October 1967)

56 A Wisconsin farm. (August 1968)

57 Midwestern farms being dusted by a snow shower, viewed from an airliner at 39,000 feet. The light bar at the left is a shaft of sunlight being reflected on the snowflakes from a pond below. The fields with stubble tend to hold snow and let it accumulate; the freshly plowed fields absorb more warmth, so the snow melts on contact—hence the checkerboard. (December 1963)

58 Contour farming at Phillipsburg, Kansas. (October 1977)

59 I was fascinated by this pattern a man with a large John Deere tractor wove at Goodland, Kansas. (October 1977)

60 The pond in the foreground reflects a dark blue sky while the tractor in the background turns up moist, rich brown earth in Iowa. (August 1966)

61 Looking straight down on an Iowa farm. The little silver buttons are the tops of silos. (July 1966)

62 Strip farming southeast of Cedar Rapids, Iowa. (July 1966)

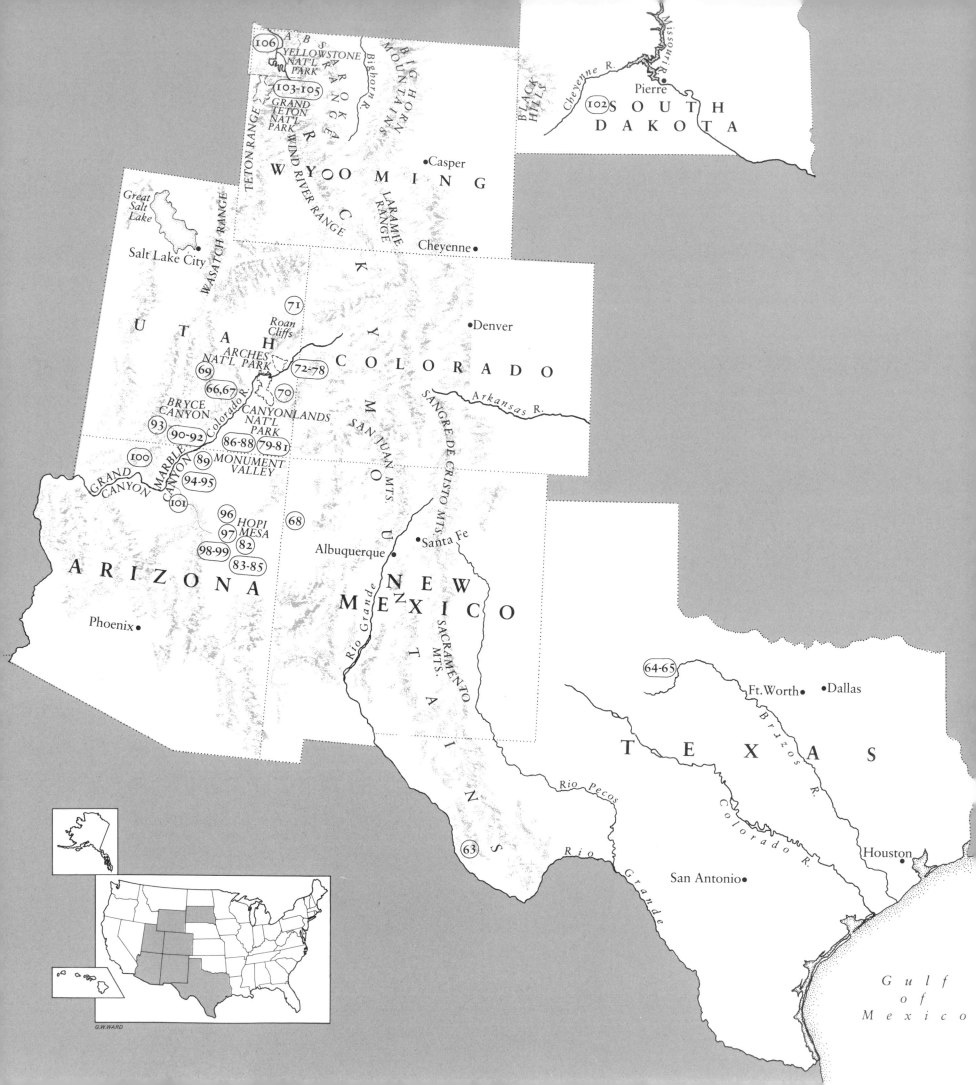

Great Salt Lake

Salt Lake City •

WASATCH RANGE

⑩⑥ YELLOWSTONE NAT'L PARK

A B S R O K A R A N G E

TETON RANGE

⑩③-⑩⑤ GRAND TETON NAT'L PARK

WIND RIVER RANGE

Bighorn R.

BIG HORN MOUNTAINS

W Y O M I N G

• Casper

LARAMIE RANGE

• Cheyenne

R O C K Y

⑦① Roan Cliffs

U T A H

ARCHES NAT'L PARK

⑥⑨

⑥⑥,⑥⑦

⑦②-⑦⑧

⑦⓪

C O L O R A D O

• Denver

Arkansas R.

Colorado R.

BRYCE CANYON

⑨③

⑨⓪-⑨②

CANYONLANDS NAT'L PARK

⑧⑥-⑧⑧ ⑦⑨-⑧①

S A N   J U A N   M T S.

M O U N T A I N S

SANGRE DE CRISTO MTS.

⑩⓪

MARBLE CANYON

⑧⑨ MONUMENT VALLEY

⑨④-⑨⑤

GRAND CANYON

⑩①

⑨⑥

HOPI MESA

⑨⑦

⑨⑧-⑨⑨ ⑧②

⑧③-⑧⑤

⑥⑧

• Santa Fe

Albuquerque •

A R I Z O N A

Phoenix •

N E W

M E X I C O

Rio Grande

SACRAMENTO MTS.

M O U N T A I N S

S O U T H   D A K O T A

Missouri R.

Cheyenne R.

BLACK HILLS

Pierre •

⑩②

⑥④-⑥⑤

Ft.Worth • • Dallas

T E X A S

Brazos R.

Rio Pecos

Colorado R.

⑥③

Rio Grande

San Antonio •

• Houston

Gulf of Mexico

G.W.WARD

Texas to South Dakota

Page 63   A lone windmill west of Marfa, Texas. (November 1975)

64–65   Sandhill cranes over the Brazos River near Knox City, Texas. (November 1975)

66   Eroded butte with snow near Caineville, Utah. (January 1967)

67   Close-up view of the same eroded butte with snow outlining the gullies. (January 1967)

68   Looking down very steeply at where a canyon cuts through mesas, only two to three miles west of Gallup, New Mexico. When I was a young man, the mesas at Gallup were often featured in Santa Fe Railway ads for the *Super-Chief*. (1954)

69   Capitol Reef, Utah, moments before sundown. Note the snow in the foreground reflecting the blue sky. (January 1967)

70   Canyonlands National Park, Utah. It is difficult to comprehend the scale of this huge eroded canyon, here locked in twenty-degrees-below-zero winter weather. The Henry Mountains, on the distant horizon, are fifty miles from the canyon. (January 1967)

71   Sunset on the Roan Cliffs, East Tavaputs Plateau, near Thompson, Utah. The scene is twenty-eight miles north of Moab. (November 1966)

72   This very long view includes the Arches National Park in Utah, looking southeast to the La Sal Mountains. The rift in the foreground clearly shows the old ocean-bed cap rock. (January 1967)

73   Arches National Park and the La Sal Mountains. (January 1967)

74–75   Looking nearly straight down on the cap rock of Arches National Park and its light dusting of snow. The trees are pinion pine and juniper. (January 1967)

76   Winter at Delicate Arch in the Arches National Park, Utah. (January 1967)

77   Just north of Delicate Arch, the cap rock has given way to erosion, forming an arch on the left. (January 1967)

78   Heavy erosion leaves standing ridges in Arches National Park, Utah. (January 1967)

79   Mexican Hat, Utah. Imagine the power of nature—the millions of tons of earth that have been eroded away from these cuts, carried by the San Juan into the Colorado River and finally, some five hundred miles away, into the Gulf of California. (August 1960)

80   A detail of the anticline at Mexican Hat, Utah. (August 1960)

81   Comb Ridge, halfway between Mexican Hat and Bluff, Utah. In the distance are the snowcapped Abajo Mountains. Coming from Salt Lake City by ox-drawn wagons, twelve pioneer Mormon families had to cross this huge anticline to settle the town of Blanding at the foot of these mountains. (January 1967)

82   The Painted Desert, northeast of Holbrook, Arizona. The whole story of the formation of the Painted Desert is told in this photograph. The towering cumulus on the right, topped off at 40,000 feet, was pounding down heavy rain and hail, eroding the desert. (June 1967)

83   A detail of the erosion in the Painted Desert. (April 1967)

84   Another detail of erosion in the Painted Desert. (November 1975)

85   Holbrook, Arizona. Both the sky and the ground here indicate strong winds to an experienced pilot. The forty-mile-per-hour surface winds were lifting sand from the dry wash to an altitude of 1,500 feet and blowing it for mile upon mile. The bright area near the center of the picture is a section on the ground that was absolutely shadowless because of its alignment with the camera and the sun. (November 1975)

86   Winter, Monument Valley, Arizona. The sun was just setting, casting the shadow of the monuments at right onto the bluff in the background at left, which was forty miles away. (January 1967)

87   Monument Valley, Arizona. (October 1966)

88   Half a sun rests on the horizon, giving this lighting to Monument Valley, Arizona. (November 1966)

89   Looking almost straight down on a snow-covered butte at Marble Canyon, Arizona. (January 1967)

90   On the right, in the shadows, Utah's Navajo Mountain. Monument Valley is fifty-five miles to the east, on the center horizon, and Black Mesa is on the horizon at right. The fury of this storm was awesome. I must give credit to a marvelous man at the office of Frontier Airlines in Page, Arizona. He was about to close for the day as the storm gathered, and I was about to take off in pursuit of late-light photographs. I asked if he would mind staying after-hours at my expense to keep the radio frequency open and inform me of changes in the wind direction and velocity at the Page airport. His immediate answer was that he would be happy to do so, but not for pay. As I flew over this rugged wilderness area, I found myself buffeted about by rough air, like a cork in the sea. The airline employee would periodically call out the wind direction and velocity at the airport. Right after I took this photograph of the clouds rolling upside down, he called out that the wind was blowing forty miles an hour right down the runway. I returned to find him waiting to hold the wing strut as I taxied back to the tie-down. I truly appreciated his help, for I could not have risked staying in the air for this picture without knowing what the increasing wind was doing at the airport, beyond my sight. (June 1967)

91   West of Wahweap, Arizona. (June 1967)

92   Lake Powell, on the border between Arizona and Utah. (June 1967)

93   Bryce Canyon, Utah, at sunrise with backlighting. (October 1966)

94–95   Navajo Indian Reservation, Arizona, with white snow on red earth and shadows from the brush. (January 1967)

96   On the left, the Hopi Mesa in Arizona. Note the cinder cones in the distance. (June 1967)

97   An eroded ridge in the Hopi Mesa country. (August 1960)

98   *Top:* A cinder cone sprinkled with light snow, near the Hopi Mesa in Arizona. (January 1967) *Bottom:* Looking straight down on the peak of the same cinder cone. Note the long shadow cast by a plug. The snow on the north face reflects the blue sky. The sagebrush is warm beige; the volcanic rock, black. (January 1967)

99   Close up, below the summit of the cinder cone, the patterns are formed by the snow (which reflects the blue sky), the sagebrush, and the black volcanic ash. (January 1967)

100   Grand Canyon National Park, Arizona. (May 1957)

101   Arizona's Little Colorado River with a blanketing of snow. The rays of the setting sun are barely catching the vertical red-faced embankment; the snow looks blue because it is reflecting the dark blue sky. (January 1967)

102   The South Dakota Badlands. This is not snow, but exposed light-colored rock where all the topsoil has been washed away. (January 1961)

103   The Grand Teton National Park, Wyoming. (October 1965)

104   Wind patterns catch the reflection of the sun at the shoreline of Jackson Lake in the Grand Teton National Park, Wyoming. (October 1965)

105   An oxbow of the Snake River in the Grand Teton National Park, Wyoming. Note the round beaver mound in the center of the lake. (October 1965)

106   A geyser at Yellowstone National Park, Wyoming. (August 1968)

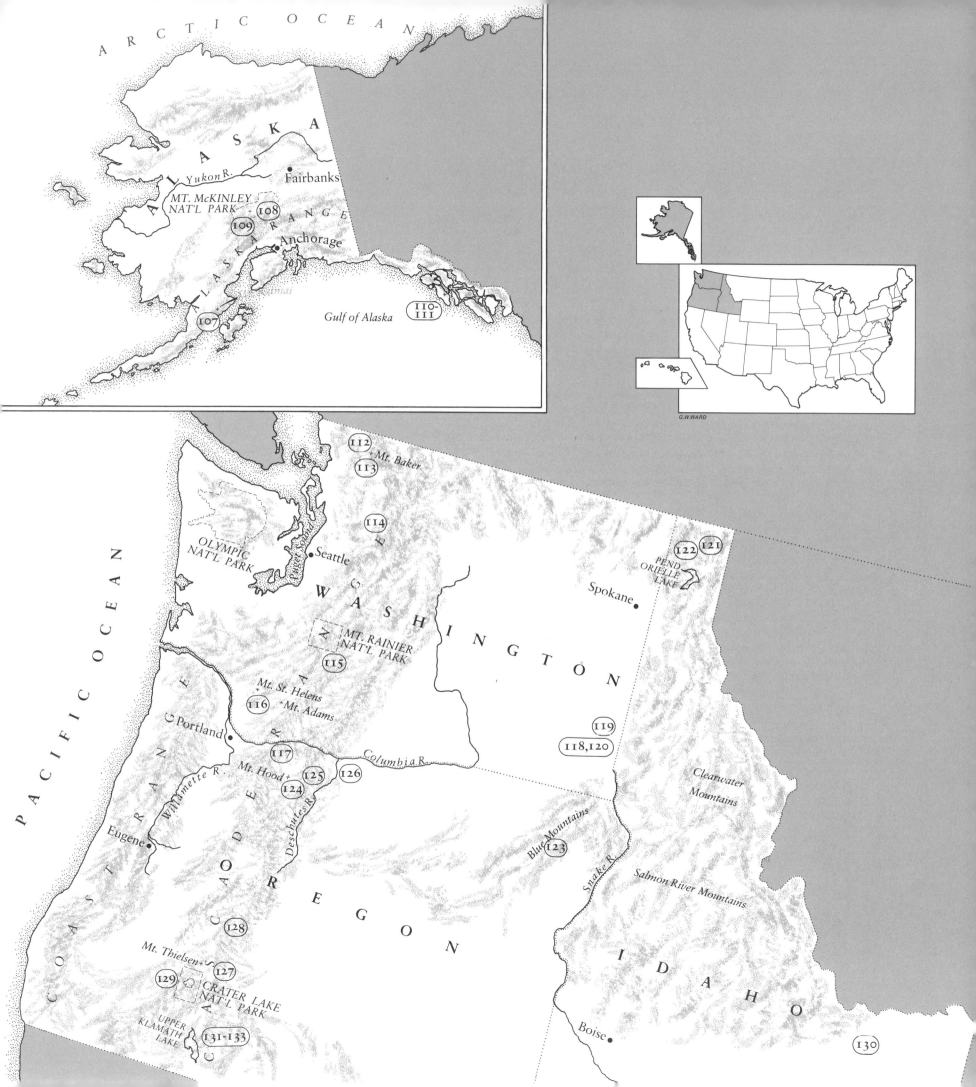

ARCTIC OCEAN

A L A S K A

Yukon R.

Fairbanks

MT. McKINLEY
NAT'L PARK

⑧

⑨

Anchorage

⑩

A
L
A
S
K
A
R
A
N
G
E

Kenai

⑦

Gulf of Alaska

⑩-
⑪

G.W.WARD

⑫

+Mt. Baker

⑬

⑭

OLYMPIC
NAT'L PARK

Puget Sound

Seattle

W   A   S   H   I   N   G   T   O   N

Spokane

PEND
ORIELLE
LAKE

⑫⑫ ⑫①

PACIFIC OCEAN

C
O
A
S
T
R
A
N
G
E

MT. RAINIER
NAT'L PARK

⑮

C
A
S
C
A
D
E
R
A
N
G
E

Mt. St. Helens
+
+Mt. Adams

⑯

Portland

Willamette R.

⑰

Mt. Hood +

⑫⑤

⑫⑥

Columbia R.

⑱⑳

⑲

Deschutes R.

⑫④

O   R   E   G   O   N

Eugene

Blue Mountains

⑫③

Snake R.

Clearwater
Mountains

Salmon River Mountains

I   D   A   H   O

⑫⑧

Mt. Thielsen+

⑫⑨

⑫⑦

CRATER LAKE
NAT'L PARK

UPPER
KLAMATH
LAKE

⑬①-⑬③

Boise

⑬⓪

Alaska to Idaho

Page 107   Mount Katmai, Alaska. (July 1967)

108   Mount McKinley, Alaska. Note the glacier at right. Flying up this canyon probably compares with flying through Yosemite in its glacial age. (July 1967)

109   A muskeg near Talkeetna, Alaska. (July 1967)

110   *Top:* Alaska's Mount Edgecumbe, with a cloud draped over its crater. Sitka is on the mainland, top center. (July 1967) *Bottom:* Silver Bay, near Sitka, Alaska, with cloud-enshrouded Mount Edgecumbe in the distance. (July 1967)

111   A detail of snow, earth, and grass on the eroded slope of Mount Edgecumbe. (July 1967)

112   A view from Glacier Peak to Mount Baker in the northern Cascades wilderness area, Washington State. The border between the United States and Canada is just beyond the right edge of the photograph. Note the notch in Mount Baker, the distant mountain on the right horizon. The picture on the facing page is a detail made in that notch. (September 1972)

113   A detail in the notch near the summit of Mount Baker reveals a gas vent that has melted through the glacial ice and snowpack. I could smell the sulfurous fumes, even at 10,000 feet, forty to fifty miles downwind. (September 1972)

114   Looking west near the Monte Cristo area of the Cascades in Washington. (August 1972)

115   In the foreground, the 14,410-foot summit of Mount Rainier, Washington. On the left horizon is Mount Adams; to its right, barely visible over the summit of Rainier, is Mount Jefferson; and on the far right is Mount Hood. All of these are major volcanoes. Mount Jefferson, which is in Oregon, is over 150 miles away. (August 1972)

116   Mount Saint Helens in Washington, nearly a decade before the major eruption in 1980. The lenticular clouds denote very high wind velocity. The sun slipped through the lower cloud layer just enough to highlight the top of the mountain. The volcano's highlighted portion is now missing, destroyed by the devastating eruption of May 18, 1980. (November 1971)

117   This sunset sky, seen from Oregon looking toward Mount Adams in Washington, reveals an interesting phenomenon. The bright spot in the sky to the right of Mount Adams is not the sinking sun, which is out of the frame of the picture, to the left; it is actually a prism spectrum effect—a rainbowlike reflection of the sun on the clouds. (July 1977)

118   A wheat field at sunrise, north of Pullman, in southeastern Washington. (July 1977)

119   After the wheat harvest at Garfield, Washington. (September 1979)

120   Trees casting shadows on freshly plowed hills near Pullman, Washington. (September 1979)

121   The Kootenai River near Bonners Ferry, Idaho. The background mountains are in Canada. (July 1977)

122   Idaho's Pend Oreille River mirroring the sky on a very calm afternoon. (June 1969)

123   A strip farm in northeastern Oregon. (June 1969)

124   The summit of Oregon's Mount Hood, 11,245 feet above sea level. This photograph was made after sunset, looking toward the east. You can see the shadow of the earth on the atmosphere in the distance and the sunset color on the high clouds many miles away. I used the slowest shutter speed of any aerial photograph that I have ever made ($^1/_{30}$ second at 1.8 on Kodachrome film). My plane was standing almost still, heading into a seventy-mile-per-hour wind. (November 1971)

125   Wheat farming in Tygh Valley, Oregon, at the base of the eastern slope of Mount Hood. (July 1977)

126   The Deschutes River in Oregon, flowing north into the Columbia River. The Columbia flows from right to left at the base of the middle mountain. The snowcapped peak in the background is Mount Adams in Washington. (July 1969)

127   Mount Thielsen in Oregon with Diamond Lake in the background. Mount Bailey is on the right. (October 1971)

128   Davis Lake, Oregon. A lava flow dwarfs the forest as it meets the lake. (September 1972)

129   Oregon's Crater Lake, in the top of an extinct volcano. (October 1971)

130   Lava fields southwest of Idaho Falls, Idaho. (August 1968)

131   Upper Klamath Lake, Oregon, during a light snow shower. (November 1971)

132–133   Mount Shasta in California, with Upper Klamath Lake, Oregon, in the foreground. Mount Shasta is seventy-five miles away in this view. (November 1971)

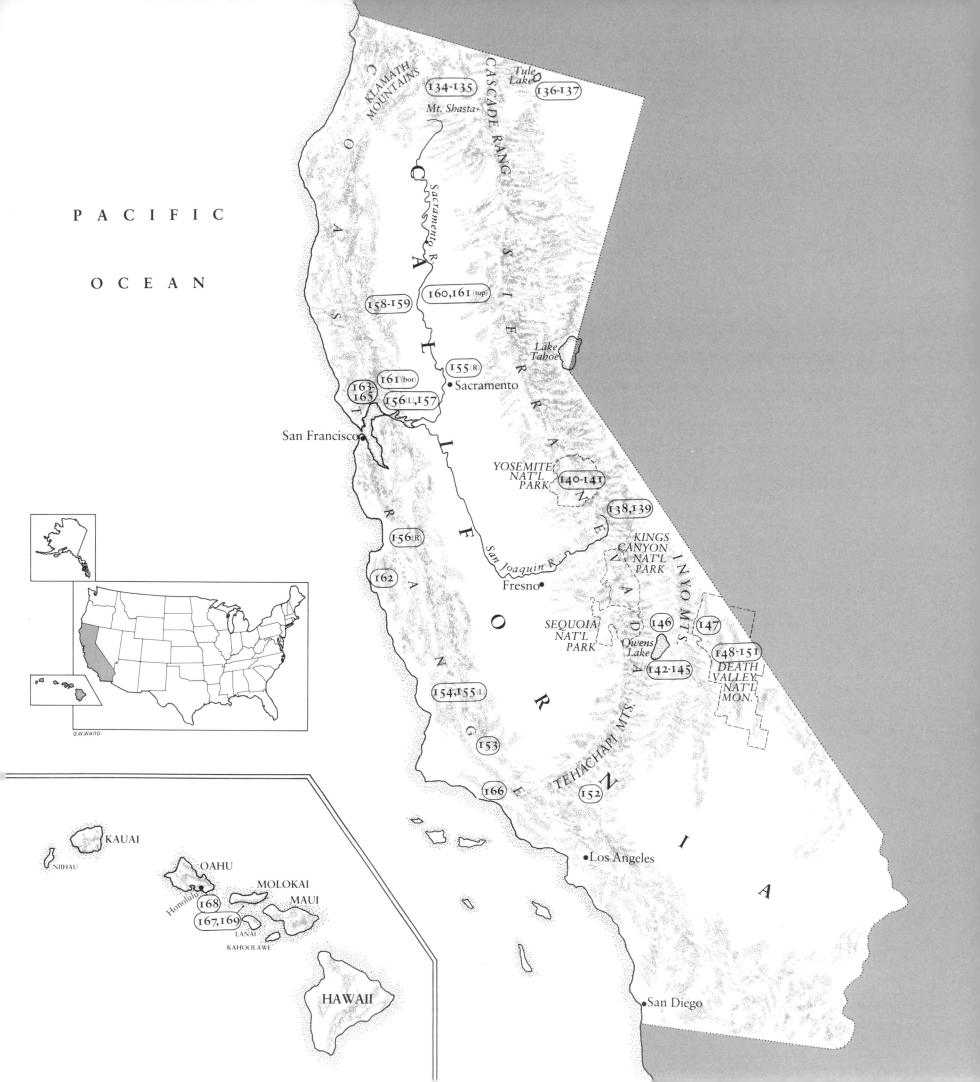

PACIFIC

OCEAN

KLAMATH MOUNTAINS

CASCADE RANGE

Tule Lake

Mt. Shasta

134-135

136-137

Sacramento R.

SIERRA

158-159

160,161 (top)

Lake Tahoe

155 (R)

161 (bot)

163-165

156 (L), 157

Sacramento

San Francisco

YOSEMITE NAT'L PARK

140-141

138,139

156 (R)

KINGS CANYON NAT'L PARK

INYO MTS.

162

SEQUOIA NAT'L PARK

146

147

Owens Lake

148-151

DEATH VALLEY NAT'L MON.

San Joaquin R.

Fresno

142-145

NEVADA

154,155 (L)

153

TEHACHAPI MTS.

166

152

KAUAI

NIIHAU

OAHU

MOLOKAI

Honolulu

MAUI

168

167,169

LANAI

KAHOOLAWE

HAWAII

Los Angeles

San Diego

G.W.WARD

California and Hawaii

Page 134 California's Mount Shasta from ten miles away. The 14,162-foot summit is covered with lenticular cloud that is forming on the right and dissipating on the left. Note the turbulence downwind, on the left shoulder, where snow and cloud are mixing. The cinder cone on the right is called Shastina. The lava flow coming toward the camera clearly shows how the cooling lava forms dikes at the edges. I headed my plane into the wind and reduced power until it remained stationary over a point on the ground. The airspeed indicator read 75 MPH. Here, to one side, the air was very smooth; upwind it was also smooth; but I would not dare to venture around to the left, to the downwind side of the mountain, under these conditions. (January 1964)

135 Detail of Mount Shasta. This is a close-up—from a thousand feet away—of the snow-covered dike near the top of the lava flow seen at the center of the photograph on the facing page. (January 1964)

136 In this sunrise scene of an Easter cross at Tule Lake in California, Mount Shasta, on the horizon, is more than fifty miles away. The area between the lake and Mount Shasta is mostly lava flow and cinder cones. (September 1967)

137 Detail of lava flow at Tule Lake, California. (January 1964)

138 The Sierra Nevada northwest of Bishop, California. (January 1967)

139 A thin sheet of wind-fractured ice reflects the sun on California's Crowley Lake. (January 1967)

140–141 Timberline pattern in the Yosemite National Park, California. (November 1956)

142 The Sierra Nevada peaks mirrored in Owens Lake. I have been making aerial photographs of Owens Lake for over thirty years. At this location the bases of the Sierra and the Inyo Mountains are only fifteen miles apart. (May 1967)

143–145 Owens Lake, California. This high desert lake bed (3,560 feet above sea level) almost completely dries out each year. The minerals wash down the mountains and turn to brine and crystals in varying designs and colors. These are just a few samples of the patterns they make. (1963; 1963; July 1971; May 1967)

146 The Inyo Mountains near Keeler, California. (May 1967)

147 Immigrant Pass, Death Valley, California. This photograph was made while flying through a light snow shower with the sun shining. Large snowflakes—about one inch in diameter—slipped past the windshield, not sticking because they were so dry. They melted on contact with the warm, sunny side of the hills and began to gather on the cool, shadow sides, where they reflected the blue sky. (January 1967)

148 The salt flats of Death Valley, California, seen from 6,000 feet above the valley floor. Much of Death Valley is below sea level. A sunset sky reflects off the lighter-colored salts; the dark areas are salt that has been stained by dust from storms. (May 1967)

149 A large sand dune in Death Valley, California. (May 1967)

150 Old-timers called these blowout dunes. Like the small ripples on the surface of sand dunes, these dunes themselves have become ripples on the hardpan desert floor of Death Valley. (May 1967)

151 *Left:* Sand dune, Death Valley, California. (1953) *Right:* Alluvium, Death Valley, California. (May 1967)

152 A large, multilayered lenticular cloud over the Tehachapi Mountains, California. (1953)

153 Soda Lake, Carrizo Plain, California. (August 1978)

154 Plowed hills near Paso Robles, California. (November 1956)

155 *Left:* A tree and its shadow on a partly plowed hill near Paso Robles. (August 1979) *Right:* Harvest design near Sacramento. (October 1975)

156 *Left:* A combine harvests grain in the Montezuma Hills near Rio Vista, California. (October 1970) *Right:* Two tractors plowing hills near Hollister, California. (November 1964)

157 Partly plowed section of the Montezuma Hills in California. I took this after a heavy fog had burned off and left moist ground—thus, the iridescent pastel color. (April 1965)

158–159 Geese over rice fields, Colusa, California. (January 1980)

160 Recently planted, flooded rice fields in northern California. (June 1961)

161 *Top:* Rice fields in various stages of growth. The water on the foreground field reflects the blue sky above California's Sacramento Valley. (May 1971) *Bottom:* Windrowed hay and a windmill, Schellville, California. (July 1975)

162 Garapata Beach, California, on the Big Sur coast. (1954)

163 Suisun Marsh, California. (April 1978)

164 Early morning fog near the Napa Airport in California. (July 1979)

165 California sunset over the north shore of San Pablo Bay at low tide. (April 1978)

166 Kelp at Santa Barbara, California. (August 1979)

167 A breaking surf pulls sand over coral on the south shore of Molokai, Hawaii. (June 1959)

168 Hanauma Bay, Oahu, Hawaii. (October 1965)

169 Coral reef off the south shore of Molokai, Hawaii. Deep water is on the left, more shallow water on the right. (June 1959)

170 The shadow of my plane on a cloud, completely encircled by a rainbow. (October 1970)

Edited by Floyd Yearout

Design and lettering by Stephen Harvard

Maps by George Ward

Copyedited by Michael Brandon

Production coordinated by Nan Jernigan

Production assistance by Amy de Rham and Geoffrey Mandel

Typeset in Sabon by The Stinehour Press, Lunenburg, Vermont

Printed by Gardner/Fulmer Lithograph, Buena Park, California

Centura Gloss paper
supplied by Lindenmeyr Paper Company, Boston, Massachusetts

Bound by A. Horowitz & Son, Fairfield, New Jersey

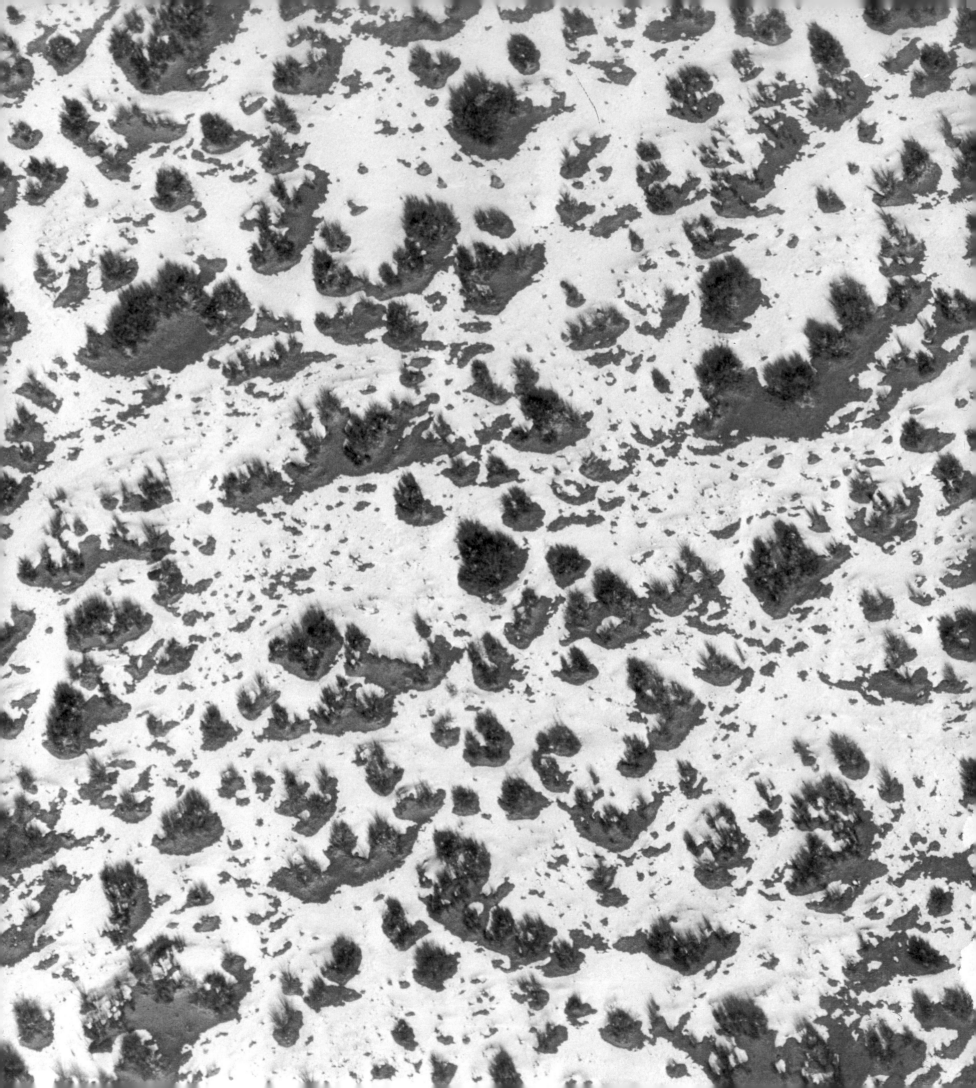